T0162742

Tam Ky

The Battle for Nui Yon Hill

Tam Ky

The Battle for Nui Yon Hill

Thomas Pozdol

iUniverse, Inc.
New York   Bloomington

Tam Ky

The Battle for Nui Yon Hill

Copyright © 2009 by Thomas Pozdol

iUniverse books may be ordered through booksellers or by contacting:

iUniverse
1663 Liberty Drive
Bloomington, IN 47403
www.iuniverse.com
1-800-Authors (1-800-288-4677)

ISBN: 978-1-4401-8783-4 (pbk)
ISBN: 978-1-4401-8784-1 (ebk)
ISBN: 978-1-4401-8785-8 (hc)

Library of Congress Control Number: 2009911915

Printed in the United States of America

iUniverse rev. date: 11/20/2009

For the men of Charlie Company 3/21 and their families

Contents

Acknowledgments

I am indebted to many people for their encouragement and assistance in putting this story together. A big thanks to Robert Russell of Patchogue, New York, who got me started on this project and helped with the initial research. Of course, a very special thanks to all the Charlie Tigers who contributed their personal information and encouraged me to pursue this endeavor.

Introduction

Reds Shell, Attack 159 U.S., Viet Sites
—Pacific Stars and Stripes

"Communist gunners and troops struck overnight at 159 targets in South Vietnam, including almost every major U.S. headquarters in country, raising speculation that a new offensive was in the works."[1]

Tam Ky is about seventy kilometers south of Danang. It is the capital of Quang Nam province, with a population of about fifty thousand. One travel guide calls Tam Ky[2] "a nondescript town on the highway between Quang Ngai and Danang." Quang Nam province lies on a coastal plain, but 72 percent of the province is mountainous terrain as one gets a few kilometers inland. The U.S. military called this coastal area the Lamar Plain. This was the northern sector of the American Division's area of operations (AO).

Operation Frederick Hill began on 18 March 1969. It involved units of the 1st Squadron, 1st Cavalry, the 196th Light Infantry Brigade, and the 5th ARVN Regiment. During this same period of time, other units of the American Division were also engaged in operations against the 2nd NVA Division and 1st

1 Pacific Stars and Stripes, May 14, 1969, page 1.
2 Vietnam Tour Packages (www.vietnamtourpackages.com).

VC Regiment. In the southern regions of the America1 area of operations, the 11th Infantry and the 4th ARVN Regiment were active in Operation Iron Mountain. The 198th Infantry Brigade and 6th ARVN Regiment engaged insurgent units in Operation Geneva Park.

On 15 May 1969, the 1st Brigade, 101st Airborne Division, along with the 1st Battalion, 46th Infantry, started Operation Lamar Plain. Elements of the 101st Airborne Division were also involved in the battle at Hamburger Hill during this time. Hamburger Hill was, of course, the most publicized battle in the press during this period. These military operations all took place during the Tet 69/Counteroffensive Campaign, which lasted from 23 February, 1969, until 8 June 1969. The men of the 3/21 received the Army Valorous Unit Award for their gallantry during this campaign.

From 5 May through 19 May, 1969, units of the 1st Squadron, 1st Cavalry were ordered to clear elements of VC (Viet Cong) from the Tam Ky area in the wake of the Post-Tet Offensive of 1969. They began an assault on a hilltop (Nui Yon Hill) where the 1st VC Regiment had overrun a critical ARVN military outpost. After the initial assault to retake the hill failed, the 3rd Battalion, 21st Infantry Regiment was air assaulted in to reinforce the 1st Cavalry. A, B, C, and D Companies of the 3/21 were committed to this operation. Echo Company 3/21 was ordered to LZ Center, and C Company 4/31 was also placed on LZ Center. The 3rd Platoon C 4/31 was sent to LZ East. On 13 and 14 May, Company C of the 3/21 met heavy resistance as they tried to move into position to assault Nui Yon Hill (Hill 94). This is the story of C Company, whose survivors simply called this operation Tam Ky.

Chapter 1
12 May 1969:
Sappers Inside the Wire

In times of war, it is desirable to be led by
a cautious and humane general

—*The I Ching*

The last quarter of the waning moon reflected off the eyes of the figure silently crouching behind a bush at the base of Hill 348. A sliver of moonlight bounced back at him off the razor wire that encircled the perimeter at the top of the hill. As 11 May 1969 slowly, quietly passed into May 12, the North Vietnamese Army (NVA) soldier's hands began to sweat as he waited for the order to attack. A bag of grenades was slung over his shoulder.

At the top of Hill 348, there was an American fire support base known as LZ Center. Most of the U.S. soldiers on LZ Center were asleep in their bunkers that night. A few stood guard around the perimeter as the lone figure with the bag of grenades and his comrades began to creep up the side of the hill. It was a little after midnight, and their slow, methodical ascent would take well over an hour.

Around 0137 hours,[3] Lieutenant James Wojczynski stepped outside the Tactical Operations Center (TOC) bunker on LZ Center. Known as Lt. Ski, he had arrived in Vietnam in August 1968. He was assigned to C (Charlie) Company as its 1st Platoon leader. In January 1969, he was promoted to executive officer (XO) of C Company. After a few months, he was assigned to the battalion as an S-3 officer. His duties, along with another officer, were to coordinate the movements of the battalion's five line companies, plot night laager sites, and log in ambush sites.

Glen Lawson and Lt. Ski

They would also monitor artillery and air strikes, making sure no one got caught in a friendly fire situation because of bad coordinates.

In ancient Vietnamese culture, the waning moon was a time of peace and the replenishing of one's strength. However, as Lt. Ski stood outside the TOC bunker, that peaceful night exploded into the reality of war as enemy mortar fire fell inside the perimeter. Looking east toward the S-4 end of the hill, Lt. Ski saw that enemy sappers had penetrated that end of LZ Center. The NVA sappers were throwing satchel charges and grenades into some of the bunkers. There were also rocket-propelled grenade (RPG) teams targeting bunkers with antennas on the south end of the

3 All the times given are taken from either battalion or brigade logs obtained from National Archive records.

hill. Immediately, he ran into the TOC bunker and sounded the siren. He then called the battalion commanding officer (CO), LTC Brandenburg, and told him dinks[4] were in the wire, to which the CO commented, "Are you sure?"

The 196th Brigade logs show that the attack started with about ten mortar rounds. This was then followed by AK-47 fire and RPG rounds. This attack took place around the S-4 and 4.2 mortar positions on the north side of the hill. It appears that the gunners were targeting the antennas on top of the 4.2 bunkers. The report goes on to state that three bunkers were damaged by RPG rounds, three by satchel charges, one 4.2 mortar tube damaged by grenades and one three-quarter-ton truck damaged by an RPG round. It is believed that ten sappers had gotten inside the wire on the northeast end of the perimeter.

The GIs on LZ Center eventually rallied and pushed the intruders off the hill by 0255 hours. Artillery was processed on the suspected enemy mortar positions with unknown results, and four NVA were engaged with small-arms fire, resulting in four NVA killed. According to the brigade logs the following equipment was captured: one B41 rocket launcher, one AK 50, twenty Chicom grenades, three AK-47 magazines, one Soviet RG42, and one Soviet F-1 grenade. Also found were a pair of wire cutters and twenty to thirty propaganda leaflets.

At 0330, the first dustoff (medevac) arrived and started to take the wounded to field hospitals. The troops on LZ Center had suffered twenty-four WIA and two KIA. Lt. Ski remembered seeing three or four dinks wearing loincloths and neck scarves and carrying bags of grenades lying dead inside the wire near the north/northeast end of the hill.

---

4 Vietnamese were often referred to as dinks, Charlie, or gooks.

The main helipad is located in the lower left. The S-4 and the 4.2 section is to the right of the helipad. TOC would be at the highest point of the hill. The sappers came up the side of the hill in the photo near the lower left.

That night, C Company was laagered southeast of LZ Center around BT161266. This would have placed the company not far from LZ East (BT132203). As they began to stir that morning to the rattle of canteen cups and the opening of C rations, a rumor began to spread that LZ Center had been overrun. Since most of the men in C Company were already seasoned by a deadly month-long operation at a place called Tien Phouc, this rumor was only partially believed. Rumors in the military were never totally believed or totally disbelieved. Since C Company had just come off of LZ Center a few days earlier, it was a little unnerving to think that there had been sappers inside the wire. Regardless of the validity of the rumor, there was business at hand that needed to be taken care of, and that was to conduct searches in an area from coordinates BT098256 to BT118267.5 If there had been a ground attack on LZ Center, this could be a bad omen for the line company. It was best to put that in the back of the mind. There had been increased enemy activity in the area the past few days. Fortunately, that day presented no out-of-the-ordinary problems as C Company patrolled its area of responsibility.

Tom "Poz" Pozdol

As the men were setting up their night laager site late that afternoon, I was called to the company command post (CP) for a briefing. My name is Thomas Pozdol. I arrived in Nam on 28 January 1969. I had taken over the first squad around 15 April 1969, from Glen Lawson. At that time, I was promoted from SP-4 to the temporary grade of sergeant, more commonly known as an acting sergeant or AJ (acting jack). After the briefing was over, SFC Paul Ikeda, who had just taken over the 1st Platoon from Lieutenant James Gordon, called me to the platoon CP to give me my instructions for the next day. The 1st Squad, 1st Platoon was to walk company point the next morning to an area out in the flatlands a few kilometers away. Walking point was one

5 All troop positions are taken from declassified government files. The letters "BT" specified a certain grid on an area of operations (AO) map. The numbers designate the exact location in that grid.

of the most dangerous jobs in Nam; walking company point was one of the most dreaded. A pace had to be set by the point squad so that a company of sometimes over a hundred men walking in column could follow without getting too spread out or bunching together. On this day, the company duty roster showed that C Company had one hundred and twenty-seven men. This does not reflect exactly how many men were actually in the field that day. Due to a shortage of manpower attributed to many factors, it has been estimated that Charlie Company had about eighty-nine men in the bush that morning. It was the responsibility of the pointman and the point squad to be in contact with the CO at all times to make sure the move went according to plans. If flanking units were sent out, which was sometimes done in the flatlands, the move became even move complicated. About dusk, I got back to the 1st Squad. I told PFC Ron Kociba that he would walk point the next day.

Ron Kociba had gotten to Nam in early February 1969. He was from Flushing, Michigan. Ron and I had survived the operation at Tien Phouc as greenseeds (new guys) and started walking point at about the same time near the end of that operation. We had also adopted a similar philosophy toward making close friendships in the bush—that was not to make any close friends in the bush. If someone in the company got killed, it hurt, but if a close friend got killed, it hurt too much. It was better not to get hurt too much. There had been nine KIA during the operation at Tien Phouc in March of 1969, and that was painful.

Ron was an intelligent man. He learned quickly and never complained. He was not afraid to speak his mind but was thoughtful in doing so. He was unlike me, who had a tendency to be impulsive. This combination often worked well for us in the field. Ron would offer insights into my decision-making process that I sometimes overlooked. Our learning curve was about the same, only we approached things in different ways. Having arrived in Nam at about the same time, we experienced many of the same things together. One of the difficulties of being a new soldier in Vietnam was that old-timers often gave greenseeds the cold shoulder. Fortunately, our squad leader, Glen Lawson, allowed us the time to develop together and at the same pace. Glen treated us like soldiers, not as fumbling newbies. Even though we kept many of our feelings inside, it was good to have someone there who was going through the same thing. Now with Lawson's absence, I was in charge. Ron accepted this and respected my decision-making process. I never sensed this from Freeman or Wolfrum, who had been in the squad longer. They accepted me as their squad leader, but I had the feeling they never completely trusted my decision making. During the Vietnam War, this lack of trust often stemmed from the ill-fated policy of rotating individual soldiers rather than complete units that were trained together. Since Ron and I had more or less trained together, there was a certain bond of trust.

The 1st Squad, 1st Platoon, left to right: John
Kwasniak, Joe Freeman, Ron Kociba

After giving Ron his instructions for the following day, I
grabbed my map and compass. PFC John Kwasniak had first
guard duty and was already in the foxhole we had dug earlier. I
pulled my poncho liner over my head. Then, I sat at the bottom
of the foxhole, turned on a flashlight, and went over the map. I
used the compass to try to get my bearings straight for the long
walk ahead of us the next day. A half hour later, feeling confident
that I knew where we'd be going the next day, I crawled out of
the hole to get in some sack time. Kwasniak was still watching
the perimeter. A short time later, at 2010 hours, the sound of
out-going M-79 rounds woke me. I asked John what was going
on. He told me that a squad on the other side of the perimeter
had spotted some moving lights and fired at them. I went back
to sleep.

Twenty-five percent of the total forces in Vietnam were draftees.[6] Charlie Company was made up of 66 percent draftees.[7] John Kwasniak was drafted in Chicago, Illinois, and arrived in Vietnam in early January 1969. He carried an M-79 for the 1st Squad. One disadvantage of a citizen army is that occasionally someone is assigned to duties that he is not cut out to do. John would have made an excellent clerk or mechanic, but he was not a field soldier. He was one of those men you had to keep an eye on at all times. This did create difficulties for other members of the squad, especially since we never had enough personnel in the bush to be a truly effective fighting unit.

The 3rd Battalion, 21st Infantry was activated from a reserve unit on 15 September 1965, and assigned to the 196th Light Infantry Brigade (LIB). In 1966, the 196th LIB was sent to the III Corps area of South Vietnam. Once there, the brigade participated in Operation Attleboro in Tay Ninh Province. The American was formed as a temporary division called Task Force Oregon in April 1967. It was to be a provisional-sized division in I Corps working out of Chu Lai. Originally, the division consisted of the 196th LIB, which was moved from III Corps, the 1st Brigade, 101st Airborne Division, and the 3rd Brigade, 25th Infantry Division. In September 1967, the American was designated as the 23rd Infantry Division. Over the next year, the division was reshaped as units were assigned to it. Finally, on 15 February 1969, it officially became the American (23rd) Division. Its mission was to assist the Marines in southern I Corps. In that area of operations, the American's orders were to deny VC and NVA soldiers from gaining a foothold in those northern provinces of South Vietnam between Duc Pho and Tam Ky. The 196th headquarters was located on LZ

---

6 *VFW Magazine*, January 2003, page 18.
7 Duty rosters were compiled every six months. The figure 66 percent is from the duty roster dated 30 April 1969.

Baldy. The 3/21 had its operations center on LZ Center. Since this division and especially the 3/21 was composed mostly of draftees and assembled under the pressure of an escalating war, the training of the troops was not always adequate to the task at hand. However, in the true tradition of citizen soldiers throughout the history of the United States of America, the men in these units accomplished their missions with the same pride, ingenuity, and tenacity of more highly trained units. This is a testament to the men of this generation who fought and died in Vietnam and not to the leadership that sent them there, and especially not to the part of the same generation who scorned the enormous sacrifice these men made in what often seemed a meaningless war.

It seemed that I had just closed my eyes when Joe Freeman shook my foot. It was my turn to stand watch, and dawn was less than two hours away. SP-4 Joseph Freeman came from Cincinnati, Ohio. He arrived in Nam in November 1968. He was a rifleman and had been rotating walking point with SP-4 Dave Classick for some time when I joined the squad. When Dave left the squad, Freeman, Ron Kociba, and I rotated walking point. Joe was quiet, tough, and reliable. He was the only black guy I ever knew who liked country music. He always carried a transistor radio in his rucksack so he could listen to the country and western music radio hour on the armed forces radio station. His favorite singer was Charlie Pride. Without a word, Freeman crawled on to his air mattress, and I crawled into the foxhole.

Placing my M-16 on the small mound of dirt built up in front of the hole, I leaned forward to scan the shadows of the trees and bushes outside the perimeter. Then I checked to see if the firing devices for the claymore mines were in their proper place. Feeling confident there was no immediate threat, my mind settled on the events that had taken place about a month before.

Glen Lawson

SP-4 Glen Lawson had been the squad leader of the 1st Squad when I joined the platoon. In early April, he began to get boils on his back, and they would break open and start to bleed every time he put on his rucksack. He had to be sent to the rear for medical treatment. Lt. Jim Gordon, who was our platoon leader at the time, asked me to replace Glen. Although there were others in the squad who had been in country longer, I had been in the military the longest, having spent an eighteen-month tour of duty with the 14th the 14th Cav in Germany. I also had above-average map and compass skills as well as training in radio procedures and small unit tactics.

The U.S. military in Germany was in a constant training mode due to the threat of a Soviet evasion. As a forward line unit, the 14th Armored Cavalry was in the field almost every month, running field training exercises (FTXs). Being a track commander of a 4.2 mortar track had honed my ability to handle situations in the field.

When I arrived in C Company, I was assigned to be a rifleman. It had been company policy not to put greenseeds in dangerously close combat situations until the platoon leader felt they could handle it. This afforded me some time to observe and learn.

After observing a few firefights, I was somewhat taken aback by the tactics used to counter enemy aggression. Many of the tactics used were contrary to what I'd been trained to do while with the 14th Cav. However, in the military, it's best to keep your mouth shut and go with the flow. That is what I did. However, the lack of using proper tactics was not always the fault of field-grade officers or squad leaders. To the men in the field, it often seemed that senior-grade officers sitting in bunkers in the rear were more interested in earning medals than in the welfare of their men. After all, in the geopolitical scheme of that era, Vietnam was just a sideshow. The real center of American military might was in Europe and the battle against the Soviets. Senior-grade officers could earn their promotions and ribbons in Vietnam and then go to the Pentagon and Europe to strut around like roosters while their men in Vietnam went home in body bags. What else could be expected from them when their first Commander-in-Chief had no clear plan for victory, and their second Commander-in-Chief was elected on a platform of an ignoble withdrawal called peace with honor. Honor maybe, but no leader should ever allow his armies to leave the battlefield without the glory of victory. Caution was not taken in laying out a strategy or proper training from the top, and this often translated into poor execution in the field. Even though officers in the field treated their men humanely, it seemed the brass were lacking in laying out an effective plan to defeat the enemy.[8]

In defense of line officers and NCOs, it was difficult to maintain a high level of combat training when your men were constantly in the bush and under enemy fire as a light infantry unit was. Moreover, it was not an easy task to teach your men to work as a team when they were in the state of constant rotation.

---

8 It is not the purpose of this book to debate the politics of the Vietnam War. However, it is important to understand that policy made in Washington often determines how decisions are made on the battlefield. Officers, NCOs, and enlisted men can only work with what they have been given. Most important, they must be given a sense of purpose. Lacking purpose made it difficult to motivate an army of conscripts whose motto was "FTA" (Fuck the Army).

The same applied to the enlisted men who had to continually get used to the abilities of new officers.

At a briefing with LTC Brandenburg prior to going into the Tam Ky area, Captain Carrier tried to inform the battalion commander that the plan to go into this area was flawed. The lieutenant colonel advised him that he had his orders and they were to be carried out. After some protest and the threat of being court-martialed, the CO of Charlie Company followed his orders. In the military, everything flows downhill.

At first, I was not keen on the idea of becoming a squad leader since I was not trained as an 11 Bravo (infantryman). I did have a combat MOS, but it was 11 Charlie (mortars). I asked Lt. Gordon if I could talk to the squad before making a decision. It turned out that no one in the squad had any objections to my becoming the next squad leader. I still felt uncomfortable taking on the responsibility of a squad leader, but Lt. Gordon convinced me that he was confident in my ability to take over for Lawson. There had been another incident a few weeks earlier that helped me in my decision to take over the squad.

Charlie Company had just completed several days of bunker guard duty on LZ Center, and a Chinook helicopter took the company to the base of Hill 352. I was feeling terrible since I had consumed too many beers the night before. The heat was oppressive and, to my embarrassment, I couldn't make it to the top of the hill without stopping to rest. After finally making it to the top, a medic gave me some salt tablets and told me to drink plenty of water. A few hours later, Lawson, who was the squad leader, asked me if I was up to walking point since the squad was going out on patrol. I told him I could handle it. The 1st Squad started down the hill with me in the lead. The sides of the trail were heavily lined with brush and trees, a perfect scenario for an ambush. A pointman always had his M-16 on fully automatic as he scanned the trail for potential danger. If something happened, there was no time to think, only react. As I came around a turn in the trail, a lone figure jumped up in front of me and to the right. He was wearing a green NVA uniform. He was running away from me through the brush. In one single swift motion, I twisted to my right, my M-16 waist high. I squeezed the trigger and nothing happened. I squeezed again—nothing. I looked down at my weapon and saw that the selector switch was in the safety position. My thumb fumbled with the switch, and I finally got it into the semi-auto position. I raised the rifle to my shoulder and fired one shot. It was too late; the dink had disappeared behind a tree and was gone. Lawson yelled to see if I were all right. I motioned for him to come up. The rest of the squad followed. John Kwasniak came up to me and said he thought I was finished. At Tien Phouc, it was one shot and the pointman was dead. We went into the brush to check the area out. I must have caught the dink taking a nap because we found a small sleeping area with his gear still in it. We found some medical equipment and documents, but there was no weapon. He must have been a medic or doctor on his way to his unit. He moved at night and slept during the day, which was common among the VC and NVA soldiers.

There was an expression in Nam, "There are two kinds of people: the quick and the dead." There were also the lucky. If that NVA soldier had had a weapon, I would have been dead. Not having to walk point was a major factor in my decision to become the 1st Squad leader.

The sun was about to break over the horizon now. I bent forward into the foxhole and lit a cigarette. I cupped it in my right hand to hide the glow and stood up again. I grabbed a handful of soil in my left hand and worked it through my fingers. Dirt in any war is an infantryman's life. He hides behind it. He crawls over it and sleeps on it. When it turns to mud, he stinks of it. This particular Vietnamese dirt began to stain your feet after a few weeks of walking through the rice paddies. It was a brownish-orange color. It took several months of baths and showers back in the States for it to finally wash out—sort of a lingering reminder of time spent in the bush. Of course, other memories lasted a lot longer. Suddenly, I heard a noise behind me and turned around.

The 3/21 Infantry set up two kinds of laager sites, one for daytime use and one as a night defensive perimeter. Most days, the laagers were set up in a different location OR set up in different locations since a light infantry unit was always on the move. Night laagers were moved to in the late afternoon. Hooches (tents) were made by snapping two poncho halves together and securing them with tent stakes and poles. Inside the hooch was an air mattress to sleep on and a poncho liner used for a blanket.

A day laager was usually a poncho liner or poncho placed on poles to afford some protection from the sun. The sides were sometimes left open to capture a breeze. Canteens were not usually left in the sun as in the above photo, but in the shade to keep the water cool.

Chapter 2
13 May 1969:
Hot LZ

The fighting appears chaotic, but they cannot be made disordered. In turmoil and confusion, they cannot be defeated.
— *The Art of War by Sun-Tzu*

Phil "Red" Crosswhite

Sergeant E-5 Phil "Red" Crosswhite had arrived in Nam in August of 1968. He was from Elixabethton, Tennessee. He was a natural born infantryman: tall, thin, and wiry. He was a leader and an expert shot with a rifle. I once saw him empty a whole magazine of M-16 rounds set on fully automatic into the bull's-eye of a target when we were at the firing range on LZ Center. He had just been appointed platoon sergeant. It was Crosswhite who had come up behind me that morning and in a low voice told me, "Stand to."

"Stand to" was the order for everyone to wake up and get ready for the day's activities. I nodded to him and pulled myself out of the foxhole. The perimeter around the night laager site started to come alive. Canteen cups were held over heat tabs to make coffee, and C-ration cans were opened. Breakfast was something simple. Usually it only consisted of a C-ration pound cake, a can of peaches, or just some crackers.

Larry Wolfrum

With a canteen cup of coffee in hand, I walked over to the 1st Squad RTO (radio trained operator). SP-4 Larry Wolfrum came to C Company in October 1968. He was from Sherwood, Ohio. He was strong and tough. He was one man who could be counted on to volunteer. Once during the operation at Tien Phouc, he and Lt. Gordon had volunteered to go out under fire and succeeded in retrieving the bodies of two men who had been killed. Another time, Wolfrum, Lawson, Freeman, and I volunteered to take some CS gas out to the 2nd Platoon after they had trapped a couple of gooks in a cave. After we had left a tree line to enter a rice paddy on the way to the 2nd Platoon, we got pinned down by sniper fire. We had to withdraw since it was important to complete our mission without delay. A second attempt along another trail finally led us to the 2nd Platoon. After completing our mission, we headed back to the company laager. On the way back, we spotted three or four gooks with weapons ditty bopping[9] along a rice paddy dike. We opened up <u>on them with</u> M-16 fire, and they went down. Discretion being

9 Ditty bopping was a term GIs used to describe the unusual way Vietnamese moved. It wasn't quite walking or running.

the better part of valor that day, we decided to continue on to the company's position rather than expose ourselves in the open paddy to get a body count of the dead gooks. These are only two examples of the many times Wolfrum did more than what was expected of him.

As I approached Wolfrum, he gave me that sort of half smile, half laugh that he was noted for. At the same time, he commented negatively on the long walk we had ahead of us that morning. I gave him a quick briefing as to what the plan was and asked him where Ike was.

Paul "Ike" Ikeda

SFC Paul Ikeda, a.k.a. Ike, had been in the army for almost twenty years. He enlisted during the Korean War and saw action at the famous battle on Pork Chop Hill. He had taken over for Lt. Gordon when Gordon went to the rear area to become the company XO. He was steady and knew what he was doing. He was also one hell of a nice guy who everyone liked. Ikeda was on the horn (radio) with the CO. He looked up at me and nodded. As I waited, I looked around the perimeter. The men of C Company were ready to move out.

Each man carried a rucksack that weighed around seventy pounds. The ruck was filled with chow for three days, extra water, claymore mines, trip flares, personal belongings, and extra ammo. On the pistol belt, each man carried a field dressing for wounds, a canteen of water with a canteen cup, a smoke grenade, and hand grenades. Some hand grenades were attached to the outside of the ruck and others were stowed away inside. Each squad member also carried some equipment that was necessary for the whole squad or the platoon—most important, extra M-60 ammo. A rifleman in the squad carried three bandoleers of M-16 ammo. The bandoleers had seven magazines each, and the magazines, although made to hold twenty rounds, were only loaded with eighteen 5.56 rounds. We had been told that the springs inside the magazines were defective and if twenty rounds were put in, they might jam the weapon. The sixteenth round in the magazine was a red tracer round. When the tracer was fired, it was almost time to reload. An M-79er wore a vest that held twenty-four M-79 rounds. Every man was a self-contained fighting unit. This was a light infantryman with the 3/21, 196th Infantry.

Ike handed the horn to his RTO and said to me, "Stand down." This meant we were to stay put. Our orders had been changed. The men began to take off their rucks. About an hour later, we were given orders to move out to an area where we were to be picked up by choppers and combat assaulted into the same area where we were to have humped (walked). This decision had come down from Battalion TOC. The CO of Charlie Company was informed about this change at 0740 hours. We rucked up again and moved out.

Capt. Ernie "Outlaw" Carrier was the commanding officer of C Company. He had taken over the company only a few weeks prior to this operation in Tam Ky from Captain William Donsbach, who had been our CO during the operation in Tien Phouc. This was to be Capt. Carrier's second tour in Vietnam. He had been a platoon leader with the 198th Infantry previously, where he served with distinction. He was now about to lead C Company into a hostile area.

Ernie "Outlaw" Carrier

Any time a grunt[10] can get a lift rather than walk, he is a happy man. I was especially happy that I didn't have to land-navigate several klicks (kilometers) over unknown terrain. However, a grunt has a sixth sense when something is about to hit the fan. The rumor about LZ Center and the sudden change in orders had made most of us a little uneasy as we waited for the birds[11] to arrive. At 1010, the birds appeared on the horizon and began to settle to the ground.[12] The Hueys arrived in a formation of three birds in a *V* shape. On this day, there were 4 Vs coming in. An infantry squad in the 3/21 consisted of five to seven men: a squad leader, two to four riflemen, an M-79er, and an RTO. A Huey could only carry this amount of men when they were in full gear, and this determined the amount of men in a squad. The 1st Squad, 1st Platoon was always in the lead bird. It was our job, along with the following two birds from the 1st Platoon, to hit the ground first and move out to secure a landing zone (LZ). Then we had to pop a smoke grenade so the incoming slicks with the rest of the company knew where to land. According to brigade records, twelve Hueys came in and then six more came in to pick up the remainder of the company. There were to be six men on each bird. However, this brigade report needs to be disputed. No one remembers that many Hueys coming in to pick us up that day. According

10 Grunt, leg, straight leg, or ground pounder were all terms that referred to an infantryman.
11 The Bell UH-1 Iroquois (Huey) helicopters were called birds or slicks.
12 *Brigade Staff Journal*, 13 May 1969, pages 2 and 3, 0740 hours and 1020 hours.

to information obtained from Capt. Carrier, there were thirteen birds that came in that morning. Most of the birds had seven men, which was the maximum amount of men in full gear that a Huey could safely carry. A few birds had six men. Record-keeping was only as good as the men doing the recording. Although most clerks tried their best, there were those who had the FTA attitude (see footnote 7).

The month of May is the dry season in this part of South Vietnam. This day was hot and sunny with very little wind, so the speed of the Hueys slicing through the air gave us some relief from the heat, which could reach over one hundred degrees during that time of the year. The relief from the heat did not last long, for within minutes of takeoff, the birds started to descend. For the past several weeks, C Company had humped the mountains and valleys farther inland. Now we could see the flatlands below us. The flatlands are where most of the productive rice paddies are located in this part of Vietnam. Within the paddies are places we called paddy islands. On these islands is where the rice farmers built their homes. These islands were covered with trees and bushes to provide shade and cover for those who worked the land. During the wet season, the farmers would work in the fields when it was daylight and retire to their hooches after dark. Some of the paddy islands were uninhabited or had been inhabited but, because of the war, were abandoned. The island that we were headed for was not inhabited. That meant that if need be, we could light up the area with weapons' fire without concern for anyone living there.

The Hueys sliced through the air, with the only sound the cracking of the rotating blades. I looked at the expressionless faces of the 1ˢᵗ Squad. Kociba, Freeman, Wolfrum, Kwasniak, and Aubrey Sample, who was temporarily assigned to the squad, all had the blank look of infantrymen as they sat looking inward. Just before the birds went in, there were no thoughts, no feelings. Maybe there was only that strange feeling in the pit of the stomach. There was no need to think about what needed to be done. Once we were on the ground, our training would kick in and there would be little need for words or thought. The birds began to descend, and the cracking of the blades became louder, but there was also another sound. It was barely audible over the sound of the helicopter blades. Suddenly, there was a thud. I could hear the chopper pilot say into his mic that it was a Hot LZ.[13] I tapped the door gunner on the shoulder and pointed to the tree line on our right. He began to spray it with 7.62 rounds from his M-60. A Huey never touches ground on a Hot LZ but hovers anywhere from a few inches to a few feet off the ground until all the infantrymen have off-loaded. Out the doors on both sides went the 1st Squad, with the squad leader out last to make sure everyone had gotten off. Boots were on the ground. The first wave of choppers was in and out; second wave in and out. The 1st Platoon was on the ground. Ron Kociba hit the ground running. He recalls that an infantryman did not like being a big target so you typically jumped out as soon as the bird got within six feet of the ground and immediately started running away from the bird. As Ron jumped, the door gunner was laying down cover fire for the 1st Squad, and we began to fan out and move toward our objective.

SP-4 Joel Pasternack was the squad leader of the 2nd Squad, 1st Platoon. Hailing from New York, he had arrived in Nam in November 1968. He recalls landing in a large open area, and we were about as far from our objective as we could be. We had to get away from the choppers as fast as we could because they were

13 A hot LZ meant there was incoming weapons' fire when the helicopters were landing.

taking so much fire from three different directions. We began running and our rucksacks dug into our shoulders with each step.

When the entire 1ˢᵗ Platoon was on the ground, SFC Ikeda pointed to the tree line on our right and pumped his fist in the air. Without a word, the 1ˢᵗ Platoon was on the move. No incoming fire. Good. Hold fire. The tree line was coming closer. No incoming fire. Hold fire. Inside the tree line, no incoming fire. I took out my compass. The 1ˢᵗ Squad had to secure an area from twelve to three o'clock—from zero to ninety degrees on the compass. I pointed, and the 1ˢᵗ Squad moved out on line to the far end of the paddy island. There was no enemy resistance. Our T-shirts were soaking wet, and sweat was pouring from our steel pots and down our faces. With throat parched, I said to Wolfrum, "First squad secure." He repeated into the radio microphone to the 1ˢᵗ Platoon CP that the 1ˢᵗ Squad had secured its position. The other squads reported in to Ike: 2ⁿᵈ Squad secure 3ʳᵈ Squad secure, gun squad secure. Ike got on the horn to the company CP and told them that the perimeter was secure and that yellow smoke was going to be popped. A yellow smoke grenade was thrown on the ground to mark our position. The other platoons in the company now knew where our defensive perimeter had been set up. Small-arms fire could be heard in the distance with an occasional heavy weapon being fired. Things began to move slower now for me. I walked over to where the platoon CP had been set up. Crosswhite informed me that two birds had been shot down during the CA, but there were no casualties.

PFC JB Evans had arrived in country in April 1969. He was from Fenton, Missouri. He carried the M-79 for the 2ⁿᵈ Squad, 1ˢᵗ Platoon. He saw one of the Hueys go down just outside the perimeter where he had set up. The door gunners were in the process of taking their M-60s and canisters of ammo off the downed bird while one of the pilots crawled between the two front seats and out the main door. The other pilot crawled out the door that was facing up since the bird was lying on its side. When the bird hit the ground, it bounced and landed on its side. The still rotating blades were torn from the rotor as they ripped into the hard earth. The helicopter crew was taking enemy fire as they departed the bird. JB and another guy started yelling to them so the helicopter crew knew where to run.

The other bird had crashed farther out into the paddy. After the bird had crashed, another Huey landed under fire to get that downed bird's crew out. One of C Company's line squads tried to get to the chopper and blow it up, but they met with too much resistance and had to return to our perimeter.

By now, all of C Company was inside the perimeter. Miraculously, there were no casualties other than from the heat and one Vietnamese Kit Carson.[14] The CO began giving orders as to how the perimeter was to be set up. I had returned to the squad, and shortly after that, Crosswhite came over and instructed me where the foxhole was to be dug and how to set up our fields of fire for what we assumed would be the coming attack on our perimeter. We took out our entrenching tools (e-tools) and began to break ground. This was not an easy task. Since it was the dry season, the ground was as hard as concrete. To make matters worse, there were huge rocks just below the surface. The heat was oppressive, and we were running low on water.

A Chinook helicopter was called in to extract the downed Huey just outside our perimeter, and another brought in a lyster

---

14 Battalion log, 13 May 1969, line 23 1110 hours: "Req dustoff gunshot wound in L arm of 1 VN w/ C Co." For whatever reason, the dustoff was cancelled at 1114 hours.

bag of fresh, badly needed water since there was no water on this paddy island. There was an old well, but the water in it stank so bad that no one was willing to drink it. Rumor had it that the gooks had thrown a dead body down the well to poison the water. Once the lyster bag was on the ground, each squad took turns filling their canteens.

Late in the afternoon, a Huey brought in an 81 mm mortar team. SP-4 Paul Reamer from Chicago, Illinois, arrived with the team. "The chopper pilot wouldn't land in the LZ for some reason. It seemed like we had to jump from fifteen feet above the ground with all of our mortar equipment," Paul recalls. Once the base plate was set and the aiming stakes put out, the mortar crew was given a fire mission to destroy the downed Huey that was still in the rice paddy. The firing procedure for indirect fire weapons was normally one long, one short, one on target. The mortar crew fired: one long, one short, and then there was a huge explosion. The gooks had decided to blow up the chopper themselves. Perhaps they were trying to intimidate us, but it didn't work. We actually thought it was kind of funny. They had saved us a few rounds of 81 mm ammunition.

Inch by inch, we dug into the hard earth. We gave up trying to dig a traditional foxhole and began to stack rocks in front of the hole to create a shallow fighting position. Ron Kociba recalls that it was so hot, dry, and rocky that digging was extremely slow and difficult. He dug as far as he could and then piled the rocks that were dug up from around the perimeter of the foxhole for as much protection as possible. More men in the company began to fall to heat exhaustion. Ron Kociba was one of the heat casualties. His face became very pale, and the world started to spin.

One of the company medics got fluids into him, and in a short time, Ron was okay. He then resumed his squad duties. In the early afternoon, a resupply chopper came in with ammo, and some of the worst heat exhaustion cases were put on it and sent to LZ Center for treatment. The afternoon dragged on, and all was quiet. Yet there was tension in the air, and everyone could feel that something was about to explode. It was only a matter of time.

1st Squad's fighting position

Rumor had it that we were to be a blocking force, and a cavalry unit and some ROK (Republic of Korea) Marines were to push the enemy into our interlocking fields of fire. After what had happened during the morning CA, being a blocking force seemed like a good thing. Initially, there may have been some truth to this rumor. In a brigade joint message to division dated 13 May, it states that C Company had established a blocking force from BT267158 to BT260152.[15] There is no mention of

---

15 Item #57 Brigade Staff Journal, 13 May 1969, item 1, page 2, paragraph c.

any ROK Marines in the area in any of the reports. Some rumors are half true.

Rumor or not, joint messages or not, sometime that afternoon, battalion called Capt. Carrier and ordered him to recon the area toward the outpost known as Nui Yon Hill, where a unit of regional forces had been forced off by a VC attack several days earlier. Someone in battalion must not have believed the rumor that there was a VC/NVA force in the area. Carrier mounted up the 2nd and 3rd Platoons and headed off in the direction of Nui Yon Hill. The 1st Platoon was to stay behind and guard the perimeter. Shortly after the patrol left the perimeter, a resupply bird came in with some chow and canisters of an ice-cold drink that resembled Kool-Aid.

The patrol had gotten about 750 meters north of the hill when the point element came upon a group of NVA soldiers laying communication wire within the tree line they had just entered. After they opened up on these enemy soldiers with small-arms fire, they began to receive intense enemy fire. The 2nd Platoon was walking point, and they must have walked up on the NVA as they were setting up a base camp or an elaborate ambush site. Even though they had not completed digging in, they were entrenched well enough to mount a major attack on the two-platoon column of C Company that had entered within their deadly range of fire.

PFC Ed Stich, who was with the 3rd Platoon, recalls, "The NVA had us dead to rights. First, there was small-arms fire. Then, they began to mortar us. We began to retreat."

Joel Pasternack, who was back in the perimeter with his 2nd Squad, saw the 2nd Platoon pouring out of the tree line in disarray.

He saw that Capt. Carrier was upset with the 2nd Platoon for not withdrawing in an orderly manner.

Ron Kociba remembers the sickening sound of an extended firefight and knew that that could only be bad news for the rest of us.

PFC Kent Nielsen joined the 3rd Platoon in January 1969. He was the machine gunner in the gun squad. When the 2nd Platoon started taking incoming fire, the 3rd Platoon gun squad was told to set up in an abandoned building. The building was torn up, but it was still solid. Not long after setting up the gun, they began to take incoming fire. The heavy-caliber rounds were ricocheting off the walls of the building and coming to a stop on the floor. They were .50-caliber rounds coming from the north, northeast. The members of the gun squad thought the rounds might have been coming from the 1st Cav tracks that were supposed to be in that direction. It was already late in the afternoon. After setting up their gun and providing a minimal amount of cover fire for the withdrawing troops of the 2nd and 3rd Platoons, the gun squad was told to retreat back into the company perimeter.

PFC Jim McCloughan was the medic for the 2nd Platoon. He had arrived in Nam in March 1969, from South Haven, Michigan. He was walking just behind the point element when they got hit. They were hit from different directions and had some wounded. McCloughan began to work on one of the wounded and handed his M-16 to SP-4 Doug Hatten, who was providing Jim with security as he patched up the wounded man. When the wounds were taken care of, Jim heard someone crying out. He crawled over to where the voice was coming from and saw SP-4 Larry Aiken and another guy sitting in a small depression in the ground. They didn't seem to be wounded but were in shock and didn't have any weapons. Jim tried to talk to them and get them to move. About five meters away, he saw an NVA soldier with an AK-47 moving toward them. Since he was without a weapon, he yelled at Aiken and the other guy to get up and move out. Jim took off in the direction where he saw some other 2nd Platoon men. When he got to their position, he looked around, and no one was following him. He looked back, but saw no one, only some NVA soldiers. The group of men he had just joined had some wounded, and he began to attend to their wounds. Suddenly, there was a loud noise and an explosion. Jim felt a pain in his legs. He looked down and his legs were bleeding, but he continued to work on the wounded. Before he could completely finish, the wounded were picked up and carried back into the perimeter where the 1st Platoon was waiting. Everything seemed to be in chaos, but they made it back to the security of the defended perimeter. Jim continued to work on the wounded. When he looked up, he saw me standing by one of the wounded who had been brought inside the perimeter.

PFC Francis Patton and I sat next to each other on the flight from the States. He was from Upper Darby, Pennsylvania. We went through in country orientation together in Chu Lai. We were both assigned to C Company and were sent out to LZ Center, where we spent a few days in the transit bunker waiting for a chopper to get us out to the bush. Once in the bush, he went to the second platoon, and I went to the first. Now, I was staring at the wound that was in his chest. He must have been pulling at the bandage that was over his wound, for it had slipped down and I could see the hole. I bent down to pull it up and over the wound again. It was a sucking chest wound, and the medic had followed procedure by putting the outer plastic wrapping over the hole and then securing it with the field dressing. Frank asked me for something to drink, and I thought about bringing him some of the cold drink that had come in on the chopper. We had been taught not to give anything to drink in such a situation. Frank looked very bad. I made eye contact with McCloughan, who was still working on the wounded, and he just shook his head. I took Frank's hand and talked to him, trying to keep him conscious until the dustoff arrived. I pondered the idea of getting him some of the cold drink because it didn't seem to matter whether he drank something at that point. He wasn't going to last much longer. Perhaps a drink would have given him a moment's pleasure. I helped to pick him up and put him in the chopper along with the other wounded. On the flight back to the States in January 1970, I looked for him, hoping he'd be there. He wasn't. I was later told that he had not made it back to the hospital alive. On the C Company morning report dated 14 May 1969, he is listed as "Decd" (deceased).

I met SP-4 Dave Bukowski only a few weeks before Tam Ky. He had arrived in Vietnam in November 1968 and was from West Islip, New York. He and I had been sent up to LZ Center along with a few other men to go in front of an E-5 board to be promoted to sergeant E-5. We spent one day and night together in the transit bunker. We talked about home, and I was very impressed with the military-type vest his mother had made for him. He was proud of that vest and wore it almost all the time. Even though Dave was a squad leader, he was walking point that afternoon. He was one of the first to be killed by enemy fire. After the dustoff left, I looked for him in the perimeter. I didn't see him. Someone told me that he was still out there in the rice paddy or tree line. On the C Company morning report dated 14

May 1969, Dave,[16] along with five other men, was listed as "Mis" (missing) (See Appendix A). There were also eight WIA that day (See Appendix B).

Capt. Carrier told Doc McCloughan to get on the dustoff before it left because of the wounds to his legs. Jim refused to do so, telling the CO that when he was in the paddy, he had looked up at Nui Yon Hill and saw the gooks pouring off of it like hundreds of ants. He informed Capt. Carrier that he was going to need all of his medics in the field that night or the next day. Jim patched up his own wounds and stayed in the field with Charlie Company.

A joint message from the 196th Brigade to the Americal Division dated 14 May reads as follows:

C/3-21, upon completion of their combat assault at 131030H, at BT267138, began receiving small-arms fire from multiple positions to their north, west, and south. C Co returned fire with small arms, artillery, gunships, and air strikes. C Co continued to receive small-arms fire throughout the day, and at 1745H, C Co received heavy mortar and RPG fire, which C Co returned with artillery. C Co was able to confirm that they killed seven VC and one NVA, while friendly losses were six U.S. WIA and five U.S. MIA.[17]

---

16 Dave Bukowski is listed on the Vietnam Memorial Wall as being with A Company 3/21. This is a clerical error. Dave appears on both the C Company duty roster and morning reports. Eyewitnesses also place Dave with C Company on 13 May. Dave was awarded the Bronze Star for his actions that day.

17 Joint message, 14 May 1969, page 4, section 3a.

2nd Platoon

Jim "Doc" McCloughan

Other members of
the 2nd Platoon

Francis Patton

Dave Bukowski

Chapter 3
The First Night Near Nui Yon:
No Sleep for C Company

Even though I walk through the valley of the
shadow of death, I will fear no evil.

—*Psalm 23*

As the sun set around 1800 hours, Charlie Company braced for an assault. The night sky was clear, and there was little wind. Dusk passed into a peaceful glow, and then it was dark, very dark. In the distance, women were screaming, and dogs were barking in a hooch area. It was apparent that the gooks were trying to harass us with this tactic. It was not clear whether they were torturing the women or just forcing them to scream out, but it would be difficult to get sleep with all the noise splitting through the night air. Just prior to the sun going down, I checked the claymores and trip flares outside our foxhole. Since there was an open rice paddy in front of us, we had clear fields of fire. If the gooks attacked during the night, we could mow them down in the open rice paddies. This was a comforting thought. As was normal, we rotated standing watch. I set the watch schedule for each man in the 1st Squad. It would be difficult to sleep when not on watch that night, but an infantryman got used to that. It was important to get some rest, if not real sleep. Earlier that day during the firefight, one of the RTOs had lost his radio. For security reasons, C Company's radio frequency was pushed up 1.15 so the gooks could not monitor our calls.[18] I double-checked with Wolfrum to make sure the change had been made on our squad radio. Finally, I settled back on my air mattress and waited for the assault that was sure to come.

At 2400 hours, the battalion log for 13 May 1969 was closed out by the following officers: James A. Wojczynski, John M. Sellers, and Stephen S. Benseman.

The activities of 13 May were summarized as follows:

2355 hours

Summary: 0110 LZ Center received S/A fire MM called on suspect VC loc. 0615 A Co received incoming arty 2 US KIA 1 VN KIA 4 US WIA 0620 dustoff req completed 0638 A B C Co's C/A'd to the Tam Ky to join D Co A B C D Co's conducted ops near Tam Ky & each Co established enemy contact A Co 2 KIA 7 WIA B Co 3 WIA C Co 6 WIA 5 MIA D Co 1 KIA 5 WIA 1 VN WIA 9 VC/ NVA BC RCN conducted opns in NW corner of Bn AO D 4/31 secured LZ Center & patrolled locally 2d platoon D 4/31 secured LZ East morale & efficiency of the Gimlets remains excellent.[19]

As 13 May passed into 14 May, it was apparent to all the men in the Gimlet line companies that danger and death loomed on the horizon. The men of the 3/21 were nicknamed the Gimlets. A gimlet was a tool used in the early 1900s to bore a hole in rock for a stick of dynamite. During the 1920s, interservice athletic games were held. The 21st Infantry so dominated the games that

18 Battalion log, 13 May 1969, line 44, 2245 hours. Reported by Lt. Ski.
19 Battalion log, 13 May 1969, line 50. This is how a typical log entry was made by both battalion and brigade.

they were said to be tougher than rock and bored through their opponents like a gimlet. If the men of the 3/21 were going to make it through this operation at Nui Yon Hill, they were going to have to live up to their nickname.

Standing watch alone in a foxhole at night was the loneliest feeling in the universe. However, it was one of the few times a soldier could put his thoughts together without interruption. Thoughts of home were usually at the forefront of one's mind during a two-hour watch. But anything that would keep a trooper awake would do. Infantrymen are normally a tolerant group of men. There are few things that raise their ire. At the top of the list that would anger your fellow soldiers was falling asleep on guard duty.

During my two-hour watch that night, I had no problems fighting back the drowsiness that sometimes comes with pulling guard in the wee hours of the morning. It wasn't so much the fear of a pending attack by the NVA as it was my own self-doubts. Thoughts of how I would perform my duty as a squad leader preyed upon my mind. I had been in firefights before even as a squad leader and did what needed to be done without any problems. Yet this thing that was bound to confront the men of C Company in a matter of minutes or hours was going to be something big. It was something not many of us had seen before. We could all feel it and smell it in the air. It was that infantryman's sixth sense again nagging at our very beings. Just hours ago, one of my friends, Francis Patton, had been seriously wounded, and may be already dead. Another friend, whom I had only met a few weeks before but respected for his leadership abilities, was now lying somewhere across the rice paddy only a hundred meters away. Dave Bukowski had seemed indestructible when I first met him. He had had more combat experience and confidence than

I had. His squad was walking point only a few hours ago, and now most of them were gone. If C Company had to move out the next day, it would be my squad that would have to take the point. Would the 1st Squad suffer the same fate as Dave's squad? Would I freeze under fire?

Suddenly, the night air was shattered by heavy-weapons fire. My thoughts were rudely brought to focus on the present danger of incoming rounds. A grunt learns early on the different sounds that weapons make when they are fired: an AK-47 sounds very different from an M-16; an RPG sounds different from a mortar round; an M-60 is distinguishable from a .50-caliber weapon. You also learn the difference between incoming and outgoing rounds.

The incoming rounds at 0350 hours that early morning were .51-caliber rounds being fired from an NVA gun team not far off. The rounds pierced the air over our heads but presented little danger to us. Men began to scramble to their foxholes as a precaution. In a few hours, it would be dawn. This had to be a precursor to the coming ground attack on our perimeter.

It was said that the VC/NVA owned the night. In reality, the night was neutral. It was difficult to pinpoint anyone's exact location at night as long as he laid low and did not do anything to give away his whereabouts. As grunts, we were taught from the onset not to give away our foxhole positions at night. Only as a last resort did you fire your weapon because the muzzle blast would let the enemy know where you were. It was drilled into your head that first you call in a fire mission from artillery or mortars, or throw your grenades, or set off the claymore mines, but you do not fire your weapon. If, as a last resort, you had to fire your weapon, it would be in short bursts with the selector switch set on semi-automatic. This was called fire discipline. The gooks did not show good fire discipline by firing the .51-caliber because it had given away their position. However, there was sometimes another reason to fire a weapon at night.

Artillery was soon called in, and the .51-caliber gun was quieted. We braced for a ground attack. It was now a waiting game. This was the simplest form of psychological warfare. They fired, we fired. They waited, we waited. The effect of all this was questionable against hard-core, experienced troops on either side, but the game had to be played. It made the generals happy. At 0420 hours, 60 mm and RPG rounds were fired on our position. In the company CP area, a handset was keyed in, "Fire mission, defcon 2." Moments later came the reply, "Round out." Company radio keyed in again, "Drop 50, fire for effect." The 105 mm rounds slammed through the air and pounded the suspected enemy positions. The gooks were probably already gone, but the ante of the cat and mouse game had just been upped. Dawn was getting closer; if the attack was going to come, it had to be now.

Ron Kociba recalls, "We spent a restless night with all kinds of noise in the distance as well as gunfire and some probing of our position, but no full-scale ground attack." Kent Nielsen recollects a very unsettled night and not much sleep. Off in the distance, the big guns of the Cav unit sent the gooks their ominous warning. If the NVA weren't coming for us, we were coming for them. The dark hours passed, and the dawn approached. The Charlie Tigers had made it through the night.[20]

---

20 Every line company had a nickname. The men of Charlie Company were nicknamed Tigers. The VC and NVA were often referred to as Charlie also. A Charlie Tiger and Charlie were not the same.

Chapter 4
14 May 1969:
Point Squad

*If you can keep your head when all about you are
losing theirs and blaming it on you …*
—Rudyard Kipling

*Early that afternoon, we moved out; everyone had good
spacing as we started over the open rice paddy.*
—Captain Ernie Carrier
CO, Charlie Company

The sun never rose in South Vietnam. It would just burst out of the east. One moment it was dark, the next it was light. The morning of 14 May exploded into heat and humidity. The men of the 1st Squad, 1st Platoon began to stir and brush the night from their eyes. Heat tabs were lit to boil water for coffee. C rations were opened. The question lingered: was Charlie still out there or had he moved out? SP-4 Joe Freeman soon found the answer. As the rest of the company was beginning to stand to, he motioned me over to him. He pointed to the tree line across the rice paddy in front of our position. Three figures were ditty bopping across the paddy horizontal to our position. I yelled at

SP-4 Ralph Hernandez, whose gun squad was in the foxhole next to ours. He couldn't see the gooks. I told SP-4 Kwasniak to put an M-79 round out there to mark where the gooks were. He didn't see them either. I grabbed the M-79 from his hands and fired a round. I'd never fired a thumper before, but as luck would have it, the round landed right in front of the three men. They staggered back a little and then started running full speed. The M-60 gunner opened up on them. They ran into the tree line across from us. A little later, another squad was sent to check out the tree line where the gooks had disappeared. They found one body riddled with 7.62 rounds.[21]

The M-60 was the best infantry weapon the grunts had in Vietnam. As long as good fire discipline was maintained so the barrel wouldn't overheat, it was a reliable gun. That could not be said for the M-16. It often jammed if not cleaned; cleaning a weapon in the field was not always easy. It was especially difficult when choppers were kicking up sand and dirt on every on-load and off-load. Grunts would always cover it with their towel whenever they on-loaded a bird to keep the dirt out. (It wasn't the barrel that was worried about so much as it was the receiver, which needed to be kept dirt free.) However, covering the M-16 for protection was not possible when off-loading in a hot LZ. An AK-47, although less accurate on full-auto than an M-16, could be carried through any field conditions and still be fired. After firing the M-79 that morning and seeing the gooks running instead of falling down, I had no respect for that weapon. The U.S.-issued LAAW (LAW) was light and accurate, but could only be fired one time. An RPG could be fired and reloaded many times. If it had not have been for artillery and air support, the

---

21 The brigade log shows C Company engaged three NVA at 0410 hours, resulting in one NVA KIA. This had to be the same incident as above. However, it could not have been at 0410 hours.

U.S. military would have been hard-pressed to have won any battle in the jungles of Southeast Asia with the tactics that were used. Needless to say, on the ground, the grunts were often outgunned and outnumbered by the enemy.

After the incident with the three gooks in the paddy, it was safe to assume that elements of the 2nd NVA Division had not left the area. They were still out there hidden in the tree islands around C Company. They were being cautious, but they were there and in large numbers. They were waiting, and the boldness of their actions translated into an ensuing battle. They were going to hit us with everything they had. The only question was when and where. Eventually, the battalion would determine the when, and the NVA commander would determine the where.

The oppressive heat of the morning and early afternoon kept both sides inactive for most of the day. Resupply choppers came in with food, water, and ammo. Occasionally a .50-caliber round or the sound of small-arms fire could be heard off in the distance or pass over our perimeter.

The hardest part of combat is often the waiting. All of one's energy is being built up inside and needs to be released, but there is only the waiting. Most of an infantryman's life is spent waiting. Finally, the waiting for C Company was over; the order was given.

Some time in the early afternoon, Capt. Carrier was given the order to move the company in column formation toward Nui Yon Hill. The men of Charlie Company were told to saddle up and move out south, southwest out across the open rice paddies.

Kent Nielsen recalls, "The decision was made to move the whole company. I was told that it was because the NVA were busily targeting our position; and, consequently, we would be hammered by mortars, heavy machine guns, and RPG as the enemy prepared to overrun our position. The plan was to move abruptly to disrupt that scenario. I was in disbelief. Most of the ground to the south of us consisted of open rice paddies. There was no cover except for the paddy dikes. We followed orders, gathered up our gear, and headed out across the now well-known paddy to the south. The 3rd Platoon was the last to leave the perimeter. I felt particularly exposed, as there was open space in front of us and nobody behind us."

The 1st Squad, 1st Platoon had point. I gave Ron Kociba his instructions as pointman. He nodded that he understood and stepped into the first paddy just outside where the 1st Squad had set up their firing position the day before. It was about 1600 hours. Freeman walked second, picking up Ron's slack. Then, it was me and Wolfrum. The rest of the company, spaced out at five meters, followed behind us.

Tactically speaking, after the events of 13 May, it would have been to our advantage to move out on line in staggered squad formations, rather than in column formation, to be at the ready to cover and fire. The gun squads could have been set in place to cover our approach to the tree line across the paddy. Using this tactic, we would have been in a position to either attack or withdraw, allowing the company commander to use his own discretion. Battalion had limited our options by ordering a column move. Now the 1st Squad had the only rational choice of withdrawing and providing its own cover fire since the rest of the company was strung out in single file.

As Ron approached the paddy island, his M-16 was on full automatic and his eyes were frantically scanning the brush for any movement. At any sign of trouble, Ron, Freeman, and I would light up the area with our 16s while Aubrey Sample (again assigned to the 1st Squad) and Wolfrum would toss in hand grenades. John Kwasniak would angle in M-79 rounds. With each step toward the brush, our hearts beat faster and our eyes moved quicker. We were inside the tree line now and had taken no incoming fire or seen any movement. The next task was to quickly search the island and then move out without hesitation across the next rice paddy. With the utmost speed, we searched left, right, up, down. We only saw trees and lots of low-lying brush, one mud-hut type structure and a very suspicious two-and-a-half-to-three-foot-deep trench line that ringed the paddy island.

There was no time to think much about who had dug the trench line or why it was there; our orders were to move out into the next paddy and keep moving until we reached the next paddy island. Ron stepped into the hard dirt of the next paddy. It was fifty to seventy-five meters wide. We got about halfway across when we saw some dinks with weapons moving in the brush. It looked as if they were running to get into position to open fire on us. Instead, we opened up on them first and withdrew back to the island we had just come from. Immediately, I informed Ike what we had seen and requested artillery support. It seemed as if a long time had passed, and finally we were told an air strike was on the way.

Joel Pasternack remembered that Capt. Carrier had called in for an air strike. As the last plane made its pass, it received AK-47 fire. After the air strike, we rucked up and moved out again.

Ron Kociba saw the jets drop a few bombs, but it was obvious to those up front that they had missed the area where we had been receiving fire minutes earlier. In any case, we were ordered to move out again.

After the last plane had dropped its ordinance, Ike gave the order to move out across the open paddy. The idea did not appeal to me at all. I tried to convince Ike and Crosswhite that the bombs had not hit their intended target and that we were going to walk right in to an enemy that was now dug in and waiting for us. We needed another air strike. At first, I refused to move the 1st Squad, stating that it was suicide. I was told that the orders had come from battalion and that I'd be court-martialed if I did not follow orders. Capt. Carrier always told his men that it flowed downhill. A few days ago, he had been threatened with a court-martial. Now it was my turn. It was flowing downhill. It was a no-win situation. By arguing with Ikeda and Crosswhite, I was trying to buy some time in the hope that someone would come to their senses. About all I achieved with this tactic was giving the NVA more time to set up their offensive plan. Finally, we decided on a plan of action that would allow me to save face. We would walk the 1st Platoon out in a *V*-type formation. Kociba would take point, Freeman a few yards off to his right. I would walk off to Ron's left and about fifteen meters behind him. The rest of the platoon would follow up in this same *V* formation. In this way, we would be able to provide cover fire for each other. This decision gave me an out. I had stepped up for the safety of my men and could follow orders at the same time.

Ron Kociba recalls, "Being pointman, I felt like I was being sent out to a certain death, but somehow you don't think about that. It's kind of hard to explain, but you have a job to do. So you put the risks out of your mind and just go about doing what is required of you. We got about three-fourths of the way across the paddy and all hell broke loose, with at least two machine guns and many rifles firing at us. Finally, they gave us the order to pull back. I tried crawling, but we were sitting ducks out in the open.

Finally, Tom Pozdol said, 'On the count of three, let's make a run for it.' On three, we got up and ran."

Everyone has a different learning curve, but at some point, an infantryman's reflexes become catlike. At almost the same time, the gooks opened up on us, the whole 1st Squad hit the dirt. No one had been hit by the initial burst of gunfire. However, lying out there in the open, we weren't going to last very long. The first thought that came to mind was that a moving target was much harder to hit than a stationary one. I got on the horn to Ike and told him I needed to get my people out of there and requested cover fire. On the count of three, we'd be on the move. Ron and I got up at about the same time. From the corner of my eye, I noticed that Freeman and Wolfrum had not gotten up to run but had stayed where they were on the ground. I had no time to say a word to them. The order had been given. I was up and hauling with a full load of gear on my back. I figured it was better to take an AK round in the rucksack than in my body.

Ron Kociba, who was also wearing his rucksack and keeping pace with me step for step, saw green tracers hitting all around us, kicking up dirt. He is convinced to this day that the decision to run for it had saved some of our lives.

Joel Pasternack saw that the 1st Squad was taking automatic-weapons fire and small-arms fire from the front. He was on the left side of the V formation with PFC William Daniels. Suddenly, they started taking incoming fire from their left. That is when he realized that we were being hit by an online assault from the tree line where the 2nd Platoon had been the day before. He couldn't remember how long he'd been lying in the paddy when Ike gave the order to return to the island we had just left. He got up and started to move. As he got up, he told Daniels to move out; he didn't. He told Joel that he wanted to help the other guys by providing cover fire for them and that he would be along in a minute. That was the last time he saw Daniels alive. Daniels never made it out of the paddy. He died there after being hit by a hand grenade.

Joel made it back to the paddy island and jumped into the trench line that ran around the island. It was chaos. He saw the 1ˢᵗ Platoon Kit Carson, Dak (see Appendix E), trying to organize the guys as they came in from the rice paddy. He then met up with one of our medics, PFC Daniel "Doc" Shea, who was attending to some guys who needed medical attention. After treating one man's wounds, Doc Shea noticed someone not far off but still in the open paddy who needed assistance. Shea ran out into the open and brought the guy back. He quickly attended to that man's wounds. Doc Shea then ran out a second time. This time, he came back with another wounded man, but he also had a wound of his own. Joel helped to apply a field dressing to Doc Shea's stomach. Shea then ran out into the paddy a third time. This time, he didn't return. Pasternack didn't see Doc Shea get hit, but his body was found in the paddy the next day.[22]

While in the trench, Joel saw one guy get hit right in his helmet with an AK round. The round penetrated the steel pot but not the helmet liner. First, Joel heard a loud bang. When he looked around, he saw the helmet spinning around on this guy's head. The guy was all right, but he said he felt like he'd been punched in the head.

Shortly after this incident, Joel and the others with him in the trench line started to receive incoming hand grenades from their left. He then realized that they were sharing the same trench

---

22 Daniel "Doc" Shea was awarded the Congressional Medal of Honor for his actions that day.

with the NVA. He saw Dak and Capt. Carrier conferring over something. Then, Dak led the men in the trench to the other side of the paddy dike and out of there.

Ron Kociba and I hit the trench line at about the same time. Somehow, both of us were unscathed. Ron saw an enemy position that was firing at us. He raised his rifle to his shoulder, aimed, and pulled the trigger, but nothing happened. He looked into the chamber of his M-16 and noticed a jammed double feed where two shells tried to enter the chamber at the same time. The rifle bolt was locked in place and could not be fired. The NVA soldier who Ron was going to shoot saw Ron and started to take aim at him, but someone killed him before he fired at Ron. Ron then proceeded to pound his rifle on the ground, desperately trying to un-jam it. Finally, about the time he thought it was going to break, the two shells fell out of the chamber. He slammed in another magazine of ammo and started to provide some cover fire for those still in the paddy.

I landed in the trench right next to SP-4 Ralph Hernandez. I asked him where everyone was. He shook his head. I took off my rucksack. I opened the top and took my map from my left leg pocket and put it in the ruck. I took out a couple of grenades and put them in the leg pocket. Then I slipped one bandoleer of M-16 ammo around my neck. At this point, Ralph fired his M-79. I looked up to see a gook running across the paddy from our left. I emptied a magazine at the NVA soldier but missed. The gook went down behind a paddy dike. Ralph put a 79 round right on top of him. Then, I heard a thud behind us. I looked around. There was a Chicom grenade spinning on top of the trench. I yelled for Ralph to get down. We both hit the bottom of the trench. Then there was an explosion, and there was a lot of pain in my legs and buttocks.

JB Evans was on the left side of the *V* when we got hit. He hit the ground and took off his rucksack when the gooks opened up on us. He moved a little but then decided to go back and get some M-60 ammo from his ruck, thinking the ammo was going to be badly needed. When he jumped over the paddy dike to open his ruck, he saw an NVA soldier in a perfectly pressed green uniform. The NVA soldier had branches sticking from his pack as camouflage. He was carrying an AK-47. He saw JB and trained his rifle on him. Quickly, JB jumped over the dike again and started to low crawl out of there as fast as he could in the opposite direction. JB could feel the AK rounds hitting the ground near him. He made it back to the paddy island and set up behind a bush. From there, he could see an NVA soldier behind a low rise in the ground with a banana tree on either side. The NVA soldier had just thrown a grenade that landed a few inches short of the trench below. JB fired his M-79 but hit the banana tree to the right of the gook. While JB was reloading, the gook threw another grenade that landed in the trench. JB took careful aim and fired. The round hit the gook dead center. PFC Darrial Carter then crawled up next to JB. As they were talking about what to do, SP-4 Jimmy McLellan came around the bush in front of them. He had his M-16 in one hand and a towel around his neck. He told JB and Carter that he had just killed a gook. At that moment, an AK round hit McLellan in the back of his shoulder and came out the front of his chest. He fell to his knees, and a white froth started to come from his mouth. He fell over dead. That's the last thing JB remembered.

Hernandez had been hit in the legs by the same grenade that hit me but was still mobile. I was mad when I got up on my knees and began to open up with my M-16 at two or three NVA soldiers running behind us from where the 2nd Platoon should have been. I emptied a complete magazine on full auto, and they kept running behind the bushes. I then threw one of my grenades in their general direction. Suddenly, I caught some movement out of the corner of my right eye coming down the trench line. It was PFC Luigi Vaccaro. He looked scared and had no weapon. I asked him where his weapon was. He told me he had lost it. I told him to go back and look for it. He said he had been hit and lifted up his T-shirt. There were two holes in the side of his stomach, each about the size of an AK round. There was no blood, only two bullet holes. I wanted to stick my finger in one of the holes to see if it was real when more men came down the trench line toward us. One was SP-4 Ken Cawdwell. His was an RTO. I asked him what was going on. He told me that the NVA were hitting us from the front, the left, and he thought from the rear also. He believed from monitoring his radio that the 2nd Platoon was ahead of us in the trench line. It became suddenly apparent what the situation was. The NVA were trying to split the company in half. They would outflank each half, encircle us, and then tear us apart. I figured if we stayed parallel to them, they could not outflank us, and we had a chance of setting up some kind of defensive perimeter. I ordered everyone with me to stay low and move down the trench until we could hook up with the 2nd Platoon. We finally reached a place where we had to leave the trench, but there was an opening in the bushes. We would have to expose ourselves to cross it. I told an M-60 gunner who was with us to provide some security as we crossed the opening. He started to run behind a tree to set up when I called for him to get back. He looked at me, confused. I pointed to the butt of his M-60, which had been blown off. I motioned for him to move out with the rest of the men. When we made it across the opening, I saw JB and Carter. Carter was yelling for Carrier, and JB had a dazed look in his eyes. I then saw Dak. He was screaming at the NVA and firing an M-79. He was in front of me, but a little off to the right. Fearing he would give away our position, I told someone to pull him down. JB reached up and grabbed the M-79 from Dak's hands. Another guy and I pulled Dak down. I told him that he was giving away our position to the NVA. In reality, Dak may have temporarily halted the NVA from splitting the company in half by his screaming and firing at them. I put my hand on Dak's chest and looked him in the eyes. He began to breathe easier. I asked JB and Carter if anyone was in charge. They told me there was an officer or at least someone with an RTO off to my left.

I don't remember who he was, but he looked scared. He was sitting with an RTO to his left. The RTO was on the horn. I tried to convince him that we needed to find a defensive perimeter and we had to stay on the move until we found one. This was not a good place to be because we had nowhere to dig in and protect ourselves. It didn't take long to convince him and we were on the move. Ron Kociba took the point again. Ron headed out toward what was then our south, southwest. He encountered two guys along the way. One of them started to say something just as he was hit by a bullet in the throat. Ron recalls that it was PFC Claude Pullen, who had only a few nights before been talking about his step-family and that his step-father had been a career military man. There was nothing Ron could do for the man, so he continued on. It was urgent that we stayed on the move. Ron finally led the way into a small diked-up area. On the side we entered from, there was a berm a few feet high. There was an opening in the middle of the area that was surrounded by smaller dikes and low-lying brush and trees. It was an almost perfect defensive perimeter. The area was roughly sixty feet wide and ninety feet long. We started to fan out to secure the area. Radio contact was made with the CO. He was told that an area had been located where we could set up a good defensive position. He was informed where we were located, and we popped a smoke grenade to mark our new position. The CO gave the order for the rest of C Company to form up with us.

At first, the mortar team that SP-4 Reamer was with thought that the point element of C Company had been hit by sniper fire. They sat down and leaned back against their rucks. It was time for a cigarette break. They had been walking near the middle of the column, not far from the Company CP, when the 1st Squad made contact with the enemy. The mortar team had just gotten inside the tree line of the paddy island when they sat down for their cigarette break. Not long after, all hell broke loose. NVA soldiers could be seen running all over the place from every direction. The mortar team was told to go back out into the paddy and move toward where a defensive position was being set up. Since the mortar tube and base plate were far too heavy to carry in such a rush, the equipment was left behind. They were not carrying any 81 mm rounds because they had used up all their ammo the day before, firing missions for the company. Paul and the rest of the mortar team made it into the perimeter unharmed. Once inside the perimeter, Paul saw Ralph Hernandez. They had served together in the gun squad when Paul was still in the bush with C Company. Paul did not drop his rucksack and was one of the few men who had all his canteens of water. Ralph was in the area that had been set up for the wounded, and he was in pain. Paul gave him some of his water. In return, Ralph advised Paul that if we were to get overrun, Paul should stick close to Dak.

PFC Jim McCloughan, who was also walking near the company CP, saw a guy get hit in the stomach. As he was treating the guy, there was an explosion near him. Jim was again hit by frags from a grenade as he had the day before while he was working on a wounded man. He and the wounded man made it into the defensive perimeter.

The first thought that entered SP-4 Harold Forth's mind, as he lay behind a paddy dike on the other side of the firefight from Jim McCloughan, was that he was all alone. Somehow, he had gotten separated from everyone else. He looked up over the dike and saw no one. He yelled to see if there was anybody around. He yelled again and again. Suddenly, he heard a voice say, "Over here." He looked up and saw Dak's head just above a paddy dike, not far off. Dak told him to come on over to where he was. Harold jumped up and ran to Dak. He was now inside the defensive perimeter that was being set up.

Sgt. Crosswhite saw SFC Paul Ikeda get up on his knees and start to wave for the men of the 1st Platoon to withdraw from the rice paddy. By getting up in that stationary position, he started to draw a lot of enemy fire. Crosswhite, Ike, the platoon RTO, and Aubrey Sample managed to find a depression in the ground and get down in it to avoid all of the incoming fire they were receiving. Two Blue Ghost Cobra gunships appeared not far off and made a run down the open paddy. Blue Ghost was the call sign for F Troop, 8th Cavalry. They provided helicopter gunship support for the 196th Infantry. The AH-1G Cobra gunship was their main attack helicopter. The Cobra carried 7.62 mini-guns, 20 mm cannons, 40 mm grenade launchers and rockets. Once the Cobras marked their targets, they lit up the rice paddy, and the NVA made a beeline for cover. While inside the trees, the gooks opened up on the gunships. The birds fired their rockets and grenades into the tree line.

When Crosswhite looked at Ike, he saw that he was in pain. Ike had been hit in both legs. He was not sure if Ike had been hit by friendly fire from the gunships or enemy fire, but Ike could not be moved. Aubrey Sample had already been wounded in the arm. Both Ike and Aubrey were patched up, but there was no place to go. Just as it was getting dark, Crosswhite sent the platoon RTO to get help. The RTO made it to the defensive perimeter, but there was no way a rescue team could be sent out to get the others. Crosswhite came to the realization that he would have to hunker down in the rice paddy with the two wounded men for the rest of the night. As soon as it was dark, he could hear the gooks moving around, trying to find their position. He dared not fire and give away where they were. They sat tight and waited. It was going to be a long night.

Back in the perimeter, I had fanned out to the right of the berm. My legs were starting to tighten up from the frag wounds, but there was no bleeding. When I got near the far end of the perimeter, I sat myself down behind a paddy dike and decided to make that my area of responsibility. I checked my ammo and found I only had a few magazines left. The selector switch on my M-16 had gotten stuck in the full automatic position. I had forgotten all about fire discipline and had used up too much ammo during the running firefight. Plus, I had left one bandoleer in my rucksack, which was still in the trench line. As I looked to my right, I could see more men coming into our position from the area where the berm was. The berm was only about ten meters from an area of heavy brush. That brush would give the NVA good cover to approach us and fire at us. The rest of the perimeter had good fields of fire since we could look out at the open rice paddies and see anyone coming. As the last of our men got in the perimeter, the gooks were hot on their tail.

From behind the brush on the berm end, they began to throw grenades in on us. One of the grenades landed very near me. I felt it explode, and my left foot went up off the ground. I looked at my boot and saw nothing unusual but felt a little numbness in the foot. John Kwasniak came crawling up to me. He had no weapon and had a field dressing on his arm. He told me he had been hit by an AK round. We said nothing more as we looked out into the open paddy in front of us. We were waiting for the upcoming attack.

Joel Pasternack was located at the far end of the perimeter away from the berm. Before dark, he heard some noises coming from his left. It turned out to be elements of the 3rd Platoon. As they left our original laager site, where the day had begun, the NVA moved in to occupy the vacated area. The last four or five men in the 3rd Platoon saw them moving in to the old perimeter. A squad was sent back to force the gooks out, but they met with heavy resistance. A gunship had come in to offer support, but the 3rd Platoon was too close to their attackers for the guns of the helicopters to give effective cover fire. The gunships left to fire their guns elsewhere along the battle lines. When the 3rd Platoon entered the defensive perimeter, Joel saw his friend from the 3rd Platoon, Ed Stich. Stich had received a variety of shrapnel wounds, and Joel helped him to calm him down and nursed him through the night. Joel was one of the few guys not to drop his rucksack in the open paddy. He still had all his food, water, and ammo. As night settled in, Joel noted that things looked pretty bad for Charlie Company.

The berm was taking the worst of the incoming, for it gave the NVA soldiers the most cover to close in on the defenders of the small perimeter. Some officers and NCOs were going around setting up our defenses for the night as the NVA were beginning their attack on us. Just to the right of where I was, a place was set up to put the wounded. Those not injured were hurriedly set up in firing positions and given their fields of fire. Most of our defenses were put up behind the berm. JB Evans and Harold Forth took up positions behind the berm. After Jim McCloughan got done working on the wounded, he too got behind it. PFCs Mike Karos and Phillip Hull set up their M-60s along the length of the berm.

Kent Nielsen was setting up his M-60 in the southwest end of the perimeter. He was right behind a paddy dike and was firing at the NVA over the heads of some men who were still trying to get out of the paddy. He was trying to get some solid footing as he fired because there was no time to set up the gun properly. That was when he was hit. The round hit him in the shoulder, just to the right of the shoulder blade, and exited his chest a little above his right breast. The bullet went right through without hitting any bone. He had no idea where the round had come from. There seemed to be only friendlies behind him. After getting hit, he was spun around and dropped to the ground. His right arm went limp. He was out of commission for the rest of the night, going in and out of consciousness.

Paul Reamer had come in from outside the perimeter after putting a claymore mine in the paddy in front of a paddy dike. He heard an NCO asking if anyone had experience with an M-60. Paul told him he had been a gunner with C Company before being assigned to 81 mm. He was handed the gun and told where to set it up. It was the same position where Kent Nielsen had been.

Just as night was falling, Joel Pasternack, still in one corner of the perimeter, was told to turn on his flashlight, with a red filter covering the light, and face it skyward. Men in the other three corners of the perimeter were told to do the same. Phil Crosswhite, who still had the platoon radio with him and was in contact with the CO, was also told to hold a red-filtered flashlight toward the sky. The flashlights were being used to mark the ground positions of our men for Spooky.

Spooky was an AC-47 gunship. The first Spooky to arrive on station that night was Spooky 11 at 1928 hours. It carried MK-24 Mod 3 flares. Each flare would last three minutes and would produce a light magnitude of two million candle power. It was also equipped with two 7.62 Gatling Miniguns. Each gun could fire at the rate of six thousand rounds per minute. When a gunship fired its guns, it looked like a lighted rope falling from the sky because of the tracer rounds. Spooky 11 began to provide C Company with cover fire as soon as it arrived on station, but the NVA pressed up hard against the besieged U.S. troops to avoid the intense fire from the gunship.

Chapter 5
The Second Night Near Nui Yon:
The Defensive Perimeter

Ask that you have a brave soul that lacks a fear of death.
—Roman poet Juvenal

The men of C Company had survived the initial onslaught of their attackers. They had been scattered and beaten back by a superior number of forces. Yet they managed to rally and form a defensive perimeter. The dark hours had now fallen over the battlefield, and C Company was without water and supplies. Most of the men had left their rucksacks in the paddy or the trench line. The ammo situation was not good. At 1920 hours, Linker 12, a resupply bird, was on its way to the company. It seemed as if the bird had been hovering over the perimeter for a long time, as it was being hit by enemy fire after it arrived over C Company's position. The first time Kent Nielsen came out of his dazed condition, he saw the supply bird lowering itself and then hovering above. There was also the sickening sound of .50-caliber rounds hitting the bird. He thought that if it had been shot down, it would have crashed right on top of us. Capt. Carrier had Jim McCloughan put out a strobe light to mark our position for the pilot. Carrier was on the horn, trying to convince the pilot to have his crew kick out some badly needed ammo and grenades. He told them to drop it near the strobe because that area was clear of ground personnel. At 2005 hours, Linker 12 left. Its precious cargo was still on board. Capt. Carrier was furious with the pilot. Kent Nielsen blanked out again from the painkillers the medic had given him.

It now became obvious to all of us on the ground that we would have to adhere to the manual and maintain precise fire discipline until we ran out of ammunition or another resupply bird could bring in supplies. I fixed my bayonet to the barrel of my M-16. The NVA were not noted for taking a large number of prisoners after a battle.

Kent Nielsen was placed with a few other wounded guys on the west side of the perimeter after he was hit. The company CP and some other soldiers were between them and the berm. He was patched up by a medic, who put a field dressing on both his entrance and exit wounds. The medic told him to lie on his right side to help stop the bleeding. After the resupply bird left, he then blanked out for a while. He was rudely woken again from his unconscious state after a Chicom grenade went off only a few feet away from him. It was very dark now. At that time, it was very clear to him that C Company was in deep trouble. He could hear some NVA soldiers on the other side of the dike talking and moving around. Out of the blue, a member of C Company scrambled up the dike and threw a grenade at them. They must have been dispersed or killed, because after that, it was quiet. Afterward, Kent was lulled back into the peace of the painkillers that had been given to him earlier.

SP-4 Thomas Rhodes, who was an RTO with the company CP, heard Capt. Carrier request an air strike around 2025 hours. Since the company was without an FO (forward observer), our

CO was calling in all the support fire that day. C Company was still in heavy close contact with the enemy. Spooky, artillery, and air strikes could not keep the enemy completely off of us, but they could help to even the odds. As long as the NVA were not allowed to mass for an all-out assault and overrun our position, we had a fighting chance. Until that night, close air support from jet fighters had only been used during the day in support of ground troops. Now our company CO was on the horn, asking for a drop danger close to our perimeter. Charlie Company was about to make history.

The battalion log concerning C Company for the night of 14 May reads as follows:

NO.	IN	Incidents, Messages, Orders
40	1810	C Co req urgent gunship support heavy contact (360°)
44	1848	Req immediate flare ship for C Co
45	1854	Spooky 11 in route to C Co loc
48	1943	C Co has 2 US KIA 7 US WIA & has confirmed from results of Blue ghost
51	1950	Linker 12 R/S to C Co
52	1953	Dustoff req to stand by for C Co
53	1945	Spooky will call his own replacement
54	2005	Linker 12 turned back (R/S C Co) C Co has enemy contact 10 meters
55	2005	Helix on station w/ C Co
56	2006	C Co still in heavy contact
57	2025	3 A/S req near vic C Co N/L
58	2041	Spooky 12 on station C Co
59	2042	Spooky 11 departed station
60	2115	Dustoff still standing by for C Co C Co still in heavy contact 10-15 meters
62	2119	C Co has 2 KIA & 7 WIA
65	2100	Spooky 11 departed station

66	2200	Spooky 12 left station
67	2200	Helix 12 still on station
68	2219	Spooky 11 back on station
74	2345	A/S & Snoopy (sic) in progress at C Co loc
76	2355	SUMMARY: A B C & D Co's conducted combat ops in BN AO Co D 4/31 secured LZ Center & patrolled locally RCN secured LZ East Co A 2/1 OPCON 3/21 eff today action today was heavy w/ all companies in heavy contact most of the day 1045 A Co rpt receiving RPG & S/A fire resulting 2-US-WIA 1805 C Co received RPG & S/A fire & 5 rds of 82 mm at 1920 C Co rpts 36-VC-KIA-BC 6-US-KIA 14-US-WIA C Co still in heavy contact at this time Spooky and Blue Ghost gunships on station since 1930 Morale & efficiency of Gimlets remains high 772400Log Closed (Lt. Benseman)

The brigade log reads:

| 61 | 1839 | C/3-21 Inf received heavy SA fire from BT254165 sustaining no US Cas. C Co returned fire with SA and Arty with unknown results. Air strikes were flown and the fighters received SA fire from BT251167 No hits or US Cas. |
| 63 | 1850 | C/3-21 Inf received heavy RPG and SA fire from BT255165 sustaining no US Cas. Fire was returned with Arty and |

| 68 | 2200 | gunships were called, with unknown results.
C/3-21 Inf report an additional 25 VC KIA as a result of action at BT255165 as of 2020hr. |

After the jets had dropped their ordinance, things quieted down. Spooky 14, which was now on station over C Company, and a shadow flare ship continued to circle around the perimeter to provide light and security. About 0200 hours, they were diverted to assist B Company, which was in heavy contact. Not long afterward, Kent Nielsen was again awakened. This time, it was by a familiar and very unfriendly sound. All the other men inside the perimeter heard the same sound; it was similar to *thoom, thoom, thoom.*

It was the sound of mortar rounds hitting the base of a mortar tube. Shortly, the mortar rounds would be coming down. If they were to come down inside our perimeter, there would be carnage. We had no foxholes. Our entrenching tools were on our rucksacks, and they were outside the perimeter. Some of the troops tried to dig holes with their steel pots, but that was futile because the ground was too hard. All we could do was lie in shallow holes or lie flat on the open ground behind the paddy dikes. The sound of the rounds of an indirect fire weapon like a mortar was *whsoo, whsoo, whsoo* as it came down. Even if you are in a foxhole, your heart starts to pound faster and faster as the sound of the falling projectiles draws nearer. Just before impact, your heart, gripped with fear, stops beating for a moment. This is the moment when you are not dead, nor are you alive. Your existence is in the balance. If the round did not come down on top of you, the air in your lungs escapes in relief. This whole event covers only a span of a few seconds. With each incoming round, the process is repeated. Lying there in the open, the men of Charlie Company waited. The first round hit the ground. It was outside our perimeter. The next round fell, and the next, and the next. They all landed outside the perimeter. We all breathed a sigh of relief. Our hearts began to beat normally.

Crosswhite, Ikeda, and Sample were still in the rice paddy. They heard the sound of the descending mortar rounds also, only they sounded much closer. Most men did not like to wear a flak jacket in the tropical heat of Vietnam. It was just extra weight to carry, added on to what was already a burden to haul around every day. However, after being wounded twice since his arrival in Nam, Crosswhite became very attached to his flak jacket. The sound of one of the falling rounds was getting closer and closer to him. Finally, it slammed into the dirt just above the hole where Crosswhite was lying. He tried to roll over, hoping to avoid getting hit. Two chunks of shrapnel ripped into the side of his flak jacket but did not penetrate it. He felt a pain in his ribs (two were broken), but there was no blood. Ike and Sample were not hit.

After the mortar barrage, they began to hit us with RPGs. An RPG has a flat trajectory. Unless it is fired on an angle, it is difficult to hit anything that is flat on the ground. This being the case in the flatlands, the RPG rounds went over our heads. Jim McCloughan and two other guys saw a gook get up on his knees just outside the perimeter. He had an RPG launcher on his shoulder and was ready to fire. All three threw grenades at him, and he fell backward without firing his weapon. When the RPG attack ended, it was followed by another mortar barrage. Had their mortar teams made their adjustments and zeroed in on us? Would the rounds fall in the perimeter this time? We braced ourselves and waited. Again the rounds fell outside the perimeter.

The last mortar round had barely hit the ground when shadows began to approach us in the darkness. The approaching enemy opened up on us with small-arms fire, and again they were tossing grenades into our tiny perimeter. Two figures were coming toward me, parallel to my position but on a slight angle. They were about fifteen meters away. I fired two short bursts. They went down. Three more figures came running from the same area. I fired again. They went down behind a paddy dike. I reached into my trouser leg pocket and took out a grenade. My index finger was in the ring. John Kwasniak, who was still next to me, told me to throw it. I pulled the pin and threw it. It landed right on top of them. Moments passed and then minutes. I waited to fire again. There was no more movement in front of me. However, there was a battle raging all around me. Everywhere, bursts of fire from AK-47s and M-16s could be heard. Grenades were exploding. M-60 rounds pounded into the attackers off to my right. RPG rounds were sailing over our position.

Joel Pasternack and Ed Stich were still together at the far end of the perimeter. They were taking incoming Chicom grenades, and one landed right between Joel and Ed. Fortunately, it was a dud. They began to throw M26 grenades back at the enemy to keep them pinned down. They were running low on grenades. Things were not looking good for Joel and Ed at this point.

Prior to the first mortar attack, Paul Reamer was sitting on his helmet, talking to a couple of other guys. When we started to get hit by the mortars, Paul hit the ground but had forgotten to put on his steel pot. He never thought about retrieving his helmet, but someone else picked it up and threw it to him. He had no idea who it was. Now that the ground assault had started,

Paul was manning his M-60. Suddenly, an AK-47 round hit his outer steel pot and put a one-inch dent and hole in it, but Paul was not hurt. The bullet was floating around between the helmet liner and outer pot. Paul couldn't hear a thing after the round hit him. However, he could feel the bullet rattling around inside the helmet the rest of the night.

As some guys to Ron Kociba's left were getting into position after the last of the mortars hit the ground, he saw an enemy soldier coming over a bank of built-up dirt less than ten feet from them. He yelled at him to get down, and Ron opened up on the NVA soldier with his M-16. The enemy soldier fell to the ground. Shortly after that, a Chicom landed only inches from Ron. He tried to crawl away to avoid the worst of the explosion. He felt the hot blast of the grenade as it went off. He was rolled over by the explosion. In his mind, he was thinking that this is what it was like to die. When he came to, he felt for his leg to see if it was still there. Fortunately, it was, and his wounds were not life-threatening. One of our medics patched Ron up as best he could, and Ron continued to man his position on the perimeter.

Harold Forth was up behind the berm, where they were getting the worst of it. The enemy was hidden behind the bushes and was throwing grenade after grenade into the perimeter. In return, Harold was throwing M26 grenades back at them. One of the incoming Chicom grenades landed at his feet. He had no time to run. He just rolled over on his side, and the grenade exploded. He was stunned, and when he opened his eyes, everything was blurry. Surprisingly, he only had a small cut on the knuckle of his thumb. He tried desperately to shake the cobwebs from his head so he could get back into the fray.

JB Evans saw the grenade land at his feet, but unlike Harold, he had no time to roll away from it. It went off, and his helmet took the brunt of the explosion. However, some of the frags penetrated the steel pot and lodged in the side of his head, near his right ear. Blood was running down the side of his head, so he took off his T-shirt and wrapped it around his head to stop the bleeding. He too shook the cobwebs from his head. Shortly afterward, he heard someone yell at him. He looked over to where the voice was coming from, and someone was motioning him over. When he got to where the guy was, he saw three heads looking over a paddy dike. He fired his M-79, and the round landed on top of the paddy dike. He reloaded and went to shoot again, and nothing happened. He tried to open his M-79 to see what the problem was. It wouldn't open at first, but finally he forced it open. When he went to close it again, it wouldn't close. Somehow the firing pin had unscrewed itself and gotten jammed in the breach of the weapon so it wouldn't close anymore.

At about this time, there was the roar of mini-gun fire from the sky above, and a lighted rope of 7.62 rounds fell from the sky. It was about 0330, and Spooky had returned to provide cover for the beleaguered troops below. I was almost out of ammo. I gave my M-16 to Kwasniak and crawled over to the company CP to see if I could get some extra ammo. There was none to be had. As I was crawling back to John, a string of rounds fired from Spooky went right through the perimeter, and some of the rounds hit the ground about two feet in front of me. I stopped dead in my tracks. After a few moments, I gathered my composure and crawled back to John. Taking the M-16 back from him, I cradled it in my arms, resting my head on the butt stock. I had about a magazine and a half of M-16 ammo left. One more ground attack and we were finished.

Chapter 6
15 May 1969:
The Bloodied Tigers Rise

After I found out that Bill Daniels didn't
make it, I was pretty shaken up.
—SP-4 Joel Pasternack

Although this be madness, yet there is method in it.
—*William Shakespeare*
Hamlet, Act 2 Scene 2

The sun did not burst onto the horizon on 15 May for C Company. It slowly crept above the tree tops. We waited and wondered if the NVA were still out there. When there was enough light, patrols were sent out to recon the area. After some time had passed, the word began to spread: Charlie had pulled out. One patrol brought in the three men who had been trapped in the rice paddy all night. They had survived the ordeal. Other patrols located the bodies of those who hadn't made it. Their six bodies were laid in a straight row with ponchos placed over them. I walked over and looked down at Joe Freeman and Larry Wolfrum. Everyone in the 1st Squad had been either killed or wounded. SP-4 Tom Rhodes got on the horn and requested dustoffs for the wounded.

The first medevac was completed at 0725. Ron Kociba and JB Evans were on it, along with six other men. As the bird took flight, Ron was afraid that it would get shot down. As the bird gained altitude, he was thankful that the ordeal at Tam Ky was over and that he'd survived. Ron would discover after surgery that he'd had over 110 pieces of frags in his body. He would spend several weeks in the hospital before returning to the bush. JB Evans would be back in the bush two days later after his wounds were treated. He would spend several more weeks in the bush and then be transferred to 81 mm mortars on LZ Center.

John Kwasniak was sent to a military hospital in Japan to have the gunshot wound in his arm treated. He would not be sent back to Vietnam. After months of treatment, he was sent Stateside and discharged from the army.

Kent Nielsen had been hit in the brachial plexus nerve system in his shoulder. He was loaded on the dustoff and slumped back against the bulwark as other wounded guys were put on the bird. He was told that the NVA had been badly beaten, but we had lost a large number of men. He was transferred from hospital to hospital for several months. He finally wound up at Walter Reed in Washington DC. Several years later, after he had heard about the fall of Saigon on the news, there was a hollow feeling of loss that was difficult to handle.

I was on the second or third medevac that came in to pick up the wounded. There were six of us on this bird. It was around 0848. This chopper hugged the tops of the trees as it sped off to the 27th Surgical Hospital in Chu Lai. We all sat on the bird; not a word was said. We were staring off into that private place that an infantryman has that's all his own. It's a place where he goes to detach himself from the cruelties of combat. It's a form of protection from the pain and the hardship and the death he has to deal with almost every day. It is an especially important place to detach oneself after a firefight like the one we'd just been through. The alternative to detachment is weakness, and weakness creates indecision, and indecision bears the fruit of defeat. The memories of the brutality of combat were still there, but they got stored in the distant reaches of the mind. The victory at Tam Ky had taken a lot out of us. There was a lot of pain, both physical and emotional. In spite of the pain, we had survived, and to continue to survive in this madness of war, we became detached. That was all that mattered for now. And in combat, the now is all that is important.

For those left in the field that morning the realities of combat were still very real. Harold Forth had ignored the wound to his thumb and stayed in the field. In a few weeks, his tour of duty would be over and he'd be back in the States. Tom Rhodes would also be on his way home in June. Joel Pasternack was pretty shaken up when he found out that Daniels didn't make it. In a few days, he would be on his way to his previously scheduled R&R in Bangkok. After Bangkok, he would spend the rest of his tour in the bush. Phil Crosswhite would be assigned to S-4 on LZ Center in a few weeks. In August, his tour of duty would be over. Capt. Carrier would help to rebuild the decimated ranks of Charlie Company and remain in command until August 1969.

Paul Reamer would remain in the field one more day before returning to LZ Center with the mortar team. He asked around to try and find out who had thrown him his steel pot the night before. He wanted to thank him. No one would admit to this thoughtful act. Paul finally chalked it up to a guardian angel being at his side.

Jim McCloughan and a couple of other guys found a dead gook with a loaded RPG launcher on his shoulder just outside the perimeter where they had thrown their hand grenades only hours earlier. Jim then started caring for the wounded again. He later passed out from exhaustion. He woke up at an aid station with an IV in his arm. The next day, he returned to C Company. He would become the company's head medic, replacing Medal of Honor winner Doc Shea.

"Charlie Company had found thirty-four NVA lying dead outside their perimeter and captured four AK-47 rifles, one RPG rocket launcher, and a large amount of NVA equipment."[23] At 0915 hours, the company engaged eight NVA about fifty meters outside their perimeter. The result of this contact was eight more NVA killed. They also captured one more AK-47 and two machine guns. At 1630, they fired at and killed one more NVA soldier. They also captured his AK-47.[24]

Over the company's battalion radio that morning, SP-4 Tom Rhodes was informed that several units of ARVNs were going to be choppered in to hook up with Charlie Company. Rhodes didn't see any birds come into the area. The ARVNs were dropped about one or two kilometers away to avoid detection and walked in to get to C Company's location. One company of ARVNs was at the C Company laager site not long after they had hit the ground. The ARVNs set up a perimeter around C Company to provide security for the exhausted troops. The rest of the ARVNs swept through the area, killing twenty-four NVA soldiers that

---

23 *Army Reporter*, 21 July 1969 page 16.
24 Brigade log, 15 May 1969, lines 20 and 37.

morning. They also found eleven enemy soldiers who were killed by U.S. aircraft.

Meanwhile, the rest of the battalion was still actively engaged in contact with elements of the 2nd NVA Division. A and D Companies, along with A Troop 1st Squadron, 1st Cav, swept south from BT237181 to BT243156. They encountered resistance from small-arms fire and RPGs. A Troop then turned north and then east. A and D Companies climbed up Nui Yon Hill meeting no resistance. They discovered a number of dead NVA soldiers in the wire around the hill and in the bombed out bunkers. From 1745 to 1800 hours, C Company was air lifted to Nui Yon Hill to link up with the other two companies. Part of B Company moved to an area north of the Nui Yon Hill to set up a night laager site. The 2nd Platoon of B Company went to Tam Ky as security for the air strip there.

At the end of the day of 15 May, the Gimlets reported seventy-nine NVA killed. In a report issued to the news media in October 1969, from the Military Assistance Command in Saigon, one hundred and sixty-two enemy soldiers were found killed in the area around Nui Yon Hill.[25]

The elements of the 2nd North Vietnamese Army Division around Tam Ky were on the run but would live to fight another battle. They would regroup with their comrades in the Que Son Valley. A few months later, they would reappear in a place called the Hiep Duc Valley, dubbed Death Valley after the bloody fighting that would take place there. Units of the 3/21 would meet their old nemesis again as they participated as part of that operation also.

---

25 Headquarters U.S. Military Assistance Command VN Report Office of Information APO US Forces 96222 Colonel C.R. Carlson, 16 May (Friday), pages 37 and 38. Press release dated October 1969

On the morning of 15 May, after two days and nights of fighting, Charlie Company had seven KIA and six MIA. The bodies of five MIAs were retrieved a few days later. Four of the men were reported as KIA on the company morning report dated 22 May. The reason for the delay in identification was that the bodies were badly burned due to the dropping of napalm. It took a few days for the bodies to be officially identified and the dog tags matched to the bodies. Six men had been left in the field on the thirteenth, but only five were recovered. Curiously, SP-4 Dave Bukowski's name does not appear on the morning report that day or any other day. No reason could be found for this omission. Perhaps it was a clerical error. The one man not recovered was SP-4 Larry Aiken.

After the compilation of all the data, C Company had twelve KIA, one MIA, and thirty WIA during the battle for Nui Yon Hill.

Epilogue

Dulce et decorum est pro patria mori
—Roman poet Horace

In retrospect, the commander of the NVA forces is not beyond criticism. He had an overwhelming superiority of forces. At the beginning of the battle on 14 May, he had the U.S. forces scattered and confused. However, he made the fatal mistake of giving the beleaguered company an out. Tactically speaking, a commander should never leave the enemy an out. The initial attack of his troops came from only three sides. Had he attacked from four sides, C Company would have been crushed before the Americans could have used their overwhelming air superiority. It is obvious he had led C Company into a trap. Yet, the trap was incomplete. This begs the question, *why?* Perhaps the U.S. battalion commanders were not the only ones guilty of tactical errors—tactical errors that cost many lives on both sides. Even if the Communist forces had annihilated C Company, they would have lost the battle. Eventually, of course, they would win the war, but at the cost of 1.1 million lives, lives that were lost to resolve a long-standing political rancor within a once united country. In their victory, the North Vietnamese people could surely ponder the words of Horace, "Dulce et decorum est pro patria mori" (It is sweet and fitting to die for one's country).

On the other hand, the men of Charlie Company, along with their 2,594,000 fellow Vietnam veterans would go home with the memory of 58,198 dead to reflect upon the words of the World War I English poet Wilfred Owen:

> *"The old lie: Dulce et decorum est*
> *Pro patria mori."*

1st Platoon on LZ East   Tom Rhodes

Ken Cawdwell, Bill Daniels, Joe Freeman PFC Pat Knowlton,
RTO 1st PLT

In full gear, ready to load on choppers

John Kwasniak, Joe Freeman, Tom Pozdol

James "Flash" Gordon

1ˢᵗ Platoon Gun Squad
Standing: Panneton, Daniels, Hernandez
Kneeling: Mitchell, Reamer

Paul Reamer in 81mm mortars

1st Platoon CP

Joel Pasternack

Chow line

Resupply bird

PRC 25 Radio

Ready for combat assualt

Appendices

Appendix A
Killed in Action(KIA)—Missing In Action(MIA)

13 May 1969

SP-4 David Bukowski

SP-4 Martin Damitio

PFC John Folger

PFC Jerome Lukas

PFC Francis Patton

PFC Allan Ward

14 May 1969

PFC William Daniels

SP-4 Joseph Freeman

SP-4 Jimmy McLellan

PFC Claude Pullen

PFC Daniel Shea

SP-4 Larry Wolfrum

13 May 1969

SP-4 Larry Aiken (See Appendix C)

Appendix B
Wounded in Action (WIA)

13 May 1969

SP-4 William Arnold

PFC Nathan Briscoe

PVT Jesse Jones

PVT Steven Lee

PFC Jim McCloughan[26]

SP-4 Manuel Sanchez

PFC Herbert Scott

VN Kit Carson (name unknown)

14 May 1969

PFC Harold Belcher

Captain Ernie Carrier

PFC Darrial Carter

PFC Richard Collins

SP-4 Barry Daniels

PFC JB Evans

PFC John Guccione

SP-4 Ralph Hernandez

SFC Paul Ikeda

PFC Ronald Kociba

PFC John Kwasniak

PFC Charles Mathews

SP-4 David Mitchell

---

26 Jim McCloughan was wounded on both the thirteenth and fourteenth of May.

PFC Kent Nielson
PFC Simpson Nitta
Sgt. Thomas Pozdol
PFC Aubrey Sample
SP-4 Roger Smith
PFC Ortestes Trush
PFC Luigi Vaccaro
PFC Warren Wishbrock
PFC Frank Woodberry

Appendix C

SP-4 Larry Aiken

After the vicious firefight that C Company was engaged in on the afternoon of 13 May, six Charlie Tigers had to be left in the field. Their bodies had lain in the sweltering heat for several days before they could be retrieved and identified. Since napalm had to be dropped to cover the withdrawal of the 2nd Platoon, some of the bodies were burned beyond recognition. They had to be identified by their dog tags. Only five bodies were recovered and identified that day. The platoon leader of the 2nd Platoon was certain that he had seen one of his men being carried away by NVA soldiers on 13 May.

Larry Aiken came from Jamaica, New York, and arrived in Vietnam in November 1968. He was assigned to the 2nd Platoon of C Company, 3/21 as a rifleman. He had been involved in several firefights during his five months with the 2nd Platoon, but none could compare to the intense battle that occurred that afternoon the 2nd Platoon ran into the NVA soldiers near Nui Yon Hill. Larry was one of the six who was left in the field that day in May. He was the one body not recovered and was listed as an MIA.

In July 1969, a communist defector surrendered to the ARVN 2nd Division. He told them that he had seen a black American soldier who was a prisoner at a heavily camouflaged NVA hospital complex seventeen miles southwest of Tam Ky.

After learning about Aiken's whereabouts, a rescue team was formed that consisted of Vietnamese Regional Forces, ARVN soldiers, Americal Division soldiers, and helicopters from the 101st Airborne Division.

An artillery fire mission consisting of 105 mm and 155 mm guns was ordered to clear a landing zone for the rescue forces since the NVA hospital was in an area of thick jungle. The big guns pounded the area, and the rescue team mounted its attack. The Communist defector led the way for the rescue team as it headed for the hospital complex about fifteen hundred yards away from where the landing zone had been blasted in the heavy jungle growth. There was no enemy resistance, but six NVA were killed and one captured. The area had about twelve huts and a large underground tunnel network. A group of ARVNs spotted Aiken about three hundred yards up a stream bed from the complex. He lay on the ground, unconscious, covered by an American poncho liner. Larry, who had suffered a broken leg sometime before or after his capture, was not mobile, and his captors tried to carry him off to evade capture. Seeing that they could not get away from the rescue team while carrying Larry, they put him down and struck him in the head. It was speculated at the time that the NVA soldiers did not want to give away their position by firing a shot. Instead, they decided to use their rifle butts.

The rescue team put together a makeshift stretcher and carried Larry into the hospital complex area. Major Gary F. Dolan of the 101st Division's 2nd Squadron, 17th Cavalry hovered above the trees, and an ARVN soldier was lowered to the ground on a rescue harness. PFC Robert Bohler, the door gunner of the Huey, was lowered down on another harness. PFC Bohler and the ARVN soldier then raised Larry up into the hovering bird.

The chopper then sped to the 312th Evac Hospital in Chu Lai. This rescue took place on 10 July 1969.[27]

On 25 July, 1969, Larry Aiken died of his wounds at the 91st Evac Hospital in Chu Lai, where he had been transferred from the 312th Evac a few days earlier. He never regained consciousness.

Ngoc Chau was the young VC medic who had defected and led the mission to rescue SP-4 Larry Aiken. He was later awarded 120,000 piasters ($1,016) and spent three months in an indoctrination camp. He said he would use the money to start a new life.[28] Meanwhile, Larry Aiken was shipped home in a body bag, the victim of a brutal war.

---

27 *Pacific Stars and Stripes*, Saigon, 14 July 1969, "Defector Shows the Way" by SP-5 Bill Elsen.
28 *Pacific Stars and Stripes*, Saigon, 28 July 1969, "Rescued Prisoner of NVA Dies While Still in Coma" by SP-5 Bill Elsen.

Appendix D
2nd NVA Division

A VC and NVA military unit was set up the same way as the Communist Party in Vietnam. That would be in cells of three. A division had approximately ten thousand soldiers. In a division there were three regiments, three battalions, three companies, three platoons, and three squads, in that order. A battalion had between five hundred and six hundred soldiers.[29]

The 2nd NVA Division arrived in South Vietnam in 1966. They were headquartered in the Que Son Valley, which was situated in Quang Nam Province. Their area of operations extended into the neighboring provinces, including the coastal province of Tam Ky. They had sustained many losses after battles with the U.S. Marine Corps and were battle tough by the spring of 1969.

During the thirteenth and fourteenth of May 1969, C Company was in contact with at least two companies of NVA soldiers from the 2nd NVA Division.[30] There were also elements of a Viet Cong Regiment engaged in the assault on C Company.

---

29 Wikipedia, "Viet Cong and PAVN Strategy, Organization and Structure."
30 *The Army Reporter*, July 21, 1969, page 16.

Appendix E

In Memory, Nguyen Dak

A Chu Hoi pamphlet used by
the Americal Division

A Kit Carson was an ex-NVA or Viet Cong soldier who defected to the United States under the Chu Hoi Program. This program allowed the defector safe conduct and to be politically reeducated and taught English. The name Kit Carson suggests that the retrained man was a scout. In reality, most were little more than interpreters. Many of the Kit Carsons were not completely trusted by the American soldiers they worked with in the bush.

For the most part, this was not true of Nguyen Dak. He was called Dak by the men of the 1st Platoon, Charlie Company who he worked with in 1968 and part of 1969. Dak was more than just an interpreter to the men of the 1st Platoon. He was someone they could rely on for advice. They could also count on Dak to fight alongside them when things got tough in the bush. Dak had a deep hatred for the Viet Cong and NVA.

I learned of this hatred one night while pulling bunker guard on LZ East. The 1st Squad was short of men and didn't have enough people to man the two bunkers that were assigned to us. I asked Lt. Gordon, who was the platoon leader at the time, for another man. Since the platoon was also short of people, he asked Dak if he'd volunteer. One of the men in the squad would not stay the night in a bunker with Dak. I assigned him to the bunker in which I was to pull guard that night. Dak and I started talking and, as it turned out, we stayed up all night talking about various things from family to the war. He told me how he had been drafted into the North Vietnamese Army. He was forced from his home when he was fifteen or sixteen years old. After training, he had to hump down the Ho Chi Minh Trail carrying mortar rounds on his back. The journey was so arduous and filled with terror that when he saw a Chu Hoi pamphlet, he decided to defect. Because he had been forced into this long trip and into the military, Dak did not have any sympathy for the Communists, now his enemy. He actually went so far as to have "SÁT CÔNG" tattooed across his chest. Dak would say it meant "Fuck the Vietcong." A more literal translation would be "Kill the Vietcong."

Dak had been the Kit Carson for the 1st Platoon when Lt. Jim Wojczynski became platoon leader in August 1968. He recalls Dak as being very loyal. Dak always looked after the American soldiers. He often volunteered to go first and check things out for us. He used to get a kick out of telling greenseeds to put the locally grown hot peppers in their food. He then enjoyed watching them run for water. When Lt. Ski left the field to become XO, he offered to give his K-Bar knife to Dak. Dak thought he was being offered a million dollars. At first, he wouldn't take the knife, but in the end he accepted the gift.

While I was in the hospital after Tam Ky, Dak came to visit me. My wounds had just reopened, and the back of my hospital gown was coated in blood. Dak was sincerely concerned about my well-being. I assured him that it looked a lot worse than it was. We talked for some time. During our conversation, he thanked me for saving his life at Tam Ky. At the time, I had no idea what he was talking about, so I gave the standard response of no problem.

After my return from the hospital, I was assigned to 81 mm mortars on LZ Center. From time to time, Dak and I would run into each other on the hill. We always stopped and talked even if for only a few minutes. One time, Dak invited me to the Kit Carson bunker on LZ Center. I sat and talked with Dak and several other Kit Carsons. I wouldn't see Dak for several months after that.

One day while in the mortar bunker, a couple guys from C

Company came running in to tell me that Dak and a greenseed were up in the day room/chapel building, getting ready to fight. They knew that Dak and I had been close and that I wasn't afraid to step in to either start a fight or end one. When I got to the day room, Dak and a young U.S. soldier were standing a few feet apart with their M-16s waist-high, pointed at each other. I stepped between them and put my hands on the barrels of both their M-16s. I chewed them both out. I told them both to save their anger and fighting for the VC. They lowered their weapons. I walked outside with Dak and told him to take it easy. He again thanked me and told me I was number one. I responded in kind.

I never saw Dak after that since I was a short-timer and would be going home soon. However, before I left the country, I heard that Dak had been seriously wounded but was recovering from his wounds. Shortly thereafter, I was told that he had left the military and gotten married.

That's the last I knew of Dak until the 196th Light Infantry Brigade reunion in July 2009, I heard from a reliable source that after the war in 1975, the Communists put Dak in a reeducation camp. Dak had been there for about five years when all contact with him was broken off. Dak's SÁT CÔNG tattoo probably did not play well with the Communists. This youthful indiscretion most assuredly cost Dak many painful experiences at the hands of the Communist cadres that ran the reeducation camp. It's a pity that Dak and many others like him had to be abandoned and left at the mercy of a ruthless form of government. Dak deserved a much better fate.

Glossary of Terms

AJ an acting jack or temporary sergeant who has the same duties as a sergeant but not the same pay

AK-47 Soviet 7.62 mm automatic rifle used by NVA and VC soldiers

ARVN Army Republic of Vietnam—South Vietnam

A/S Air strike

CA combat assault, usually by troops dropped from helicopters

CAV Cavalry—Air Cav units used helicopters; armored cav units used M-113 armored personnel carriers

Chicom Chinese communist

claymore command detonated antipersonnel mine

CO commanding officer

Cobra attack helicopter AH-1G

CP command post

day laager site Defensive perimeter set up for day use

defcon defense readiness condition—a pre-set location to call in an artillery or mortar fire mission in support of a laager site

dustoff UH-1 Huey medevac helicopter

E-tool entrenching tool used to dig foxholes

FO	forward observer
FTX	field-training exercise
greenseed	new soldier with little or no combat experience
Helix	call sign for an Air Force forward air controller
hooch	any building or structure that provided shelter
Hot LZ	landing zone where helicopters are receiving incoming fire
KIA	killed in action
klick	kilometer
to laager	to set up a defensive perimeter for protection from enemy attack
LAWA	66 mm light anti-armor weapon used to blow up enemy bunkers, sometimes LAAW
LTC	lieutenant colonel
LZ	landing zone, an area for helicopters to land
M-79A	40 mm grenade launcher
M-16A	5.56 mm assault rifle
M-60A	7.62 mm machine gun
MIA	missing in action
MOS	military occupation specialties, a job description. For example, 11B is infantry; 11C is mortars
NCO	noncommissioned officer
night laager	a night defensive perimeter
NVA	North Vietnamese Army
RPG	rocket-propelled grenade
RTO	radio-trained operator or radio telephone operator
S-3	operations
S-4	logistics
SA	small-arms fire

sapper	an NVA or VC soldier trained to infiltrate a defensive perimeter
slick	UH-1 Huey
Spooky	AC-47 gunship
TOC	tactical operations center
trip flare	an M49A1 flare activated by a trip wire that gives early warning if enemy troops are trying to infiltrate the perimeter
VC	Viet Cong
WIA	wounded in action
XO	executive officer, second in command

Maps

13 May—Combat Assault and Patrol

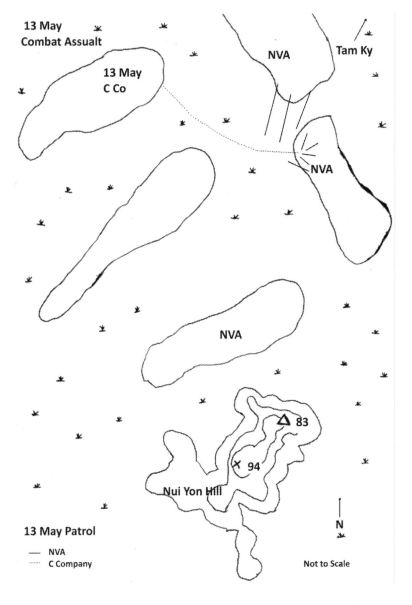

13 May
Combat Assualt

13 May
C Co

NVA

Tam Ky

NVA

NVA

83

94

Nui Yon Hill

N

13 May Patrol

— NVA
...... C Company

Not to Scale

14 May—Patrol

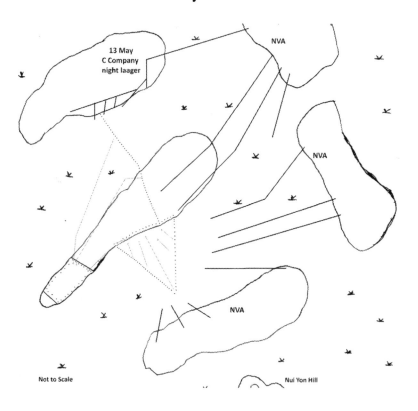

Bibliography

Department of Defense Documents

- Battalion log S2/S3 Section, 3/21 Infantry Gimlets, 12 May–15 May 1969
- Brigade log S2/S3 Section, 196th Infantry, LZ Baldy, 12 May–15 May 1969
- Brigade Staff Journal, 196th Infantry, LZ Baldy, 12 May–15 May 1969
- Duty roster, C Company 3/21, 30 April 1969
- Morning report, C Company 3/21, 12 May–15May 1969
- Press release, Headquarters U.S. Military Assistance Command VN, October 1969

Newspapers

- *Army Reporter*, 21 July 1969 page 16
- *Pacific Stars and Stripes*, 14 May 1969, page 1
- *Pacific Stars and Stripes*, Saigon edition, 14 July 1969 and 28 July 1969

Magazines

- *VFW Magazine,* 23 January 2003, page 18

Web Sites

- Vietnam Tour Package, (www.vietnamtourpackage.com)
- Wikipedia, "Viet Cong and PVN Strategy, Organization and Structure"